Melody, Lyrics and Simplified Chords

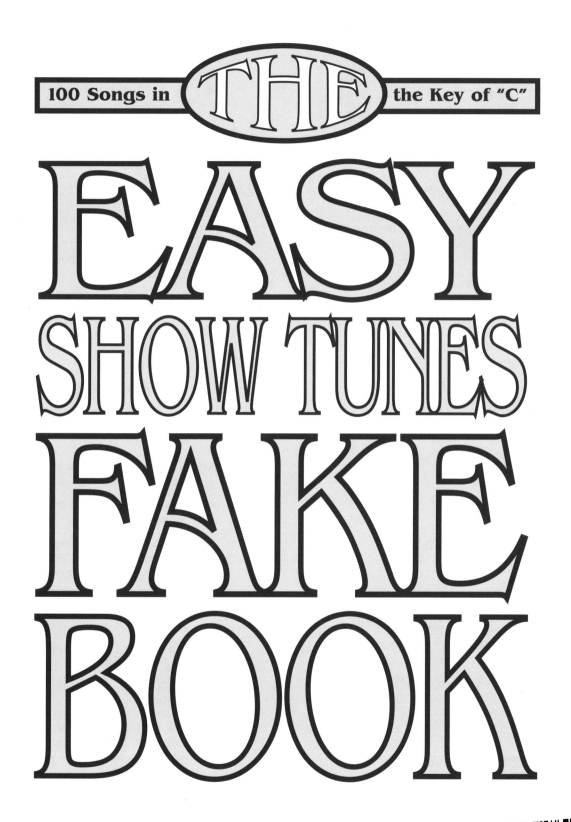

100 Songs in THE the Key of "C"

THE EASY SHOW TUNES FAKE BOOK

ISBN-13: 978-1-4234-2779-7
ISBN-10: 1-4234-2779-3

HAL•LEONARD®
CORPORATION
7777 W. BLUEMOUND RD. P.O. BOX 13819 MILWAUKEE, WI 53213

Visit Hal Leonard Online at
www.halleonard.com

THE EASY SHOW TUNES FAKE BOOK

CONTENTS

INTRODUCTION

What Is a Fake Book?

A fake book has one-line music notation consisting of melody, lyrics and chord symbols. This lead sheet format is a "musical shorthand" which is an invaluable resource for all musicians—hobbyists to professionals.

Here's how *The Easy Show Tunes Fake Book* differs from most standard fake books:

- All songs are in the key of C.

- Many of the melodies have been simplified.

- Only five basic chord types are used—major, minor, seventh, diminished and augmented.

- The music notation is larger for ease of reading.

In the event that you haven't used chord symbols to create accompaniment, or your experience is limited, a chord speller chart is included at the back of the book to help you get started.

Have fun!

AS IF WE NEVER SAID GOODBYE

from SUNSET BOULEVARD

Music by ANDREW LLOYD WEBBER
Lyrics by DON BLACK and CHRISTOPHER HAMPTON,
with contributions by AMY POWERS

Moderately

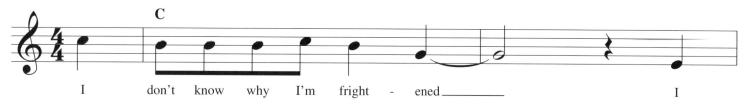

I don't know why I'm fright - ened _____ I

know my way a - round here. _____ The card - board trees, the

paint - ed seas, _____ the sound here. _____ Yes, a

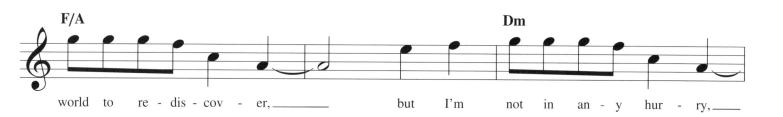

world to re - dis - cov - er, _____ but I'm not in an - y hur - ry, ___

___ and I need a mo - ment. The

whis - pered con - ver - sa - tions _____ in o - ver - crowd - ed hall - ways, _

the at - mos - phere___ as thrill - ing here___ as

al - ways.___ Feel the ear - ly morn - ing mad - ness,___

___ feel the mag - ic in the mak - ing.___ Why,

ev - ery - thing's as if we nev - er said good - bye.___

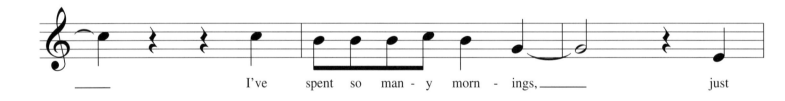

____ I've spent so man - y morn - ings,___ just

try - ing to re - sist you.___ I'm trem - bling now,___ you

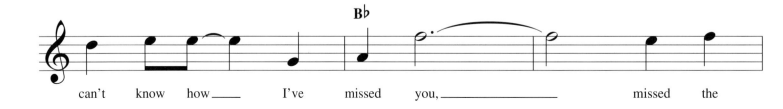

can't know how___ I've missed you,___ missed the

fair - y - tale ad - ven - tures_____ in this ev - er - spin - ning play - ground._

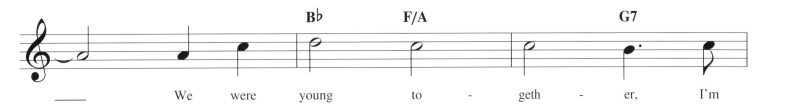

____ We were young to - geth - er, I'm

com - ing out of make - up, the light's al - read - y burn - ing, ___

____ not long un - til_____ the cam - eras will___ start

turn - ing,_____ and the ear - ly morn - ing mad - ness, ___

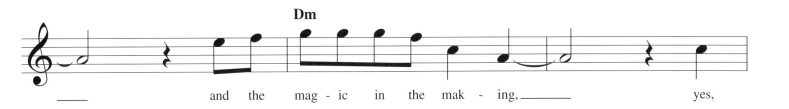

____ and the mag - ic in the mak - ing,_____ yes,

ev - ery-thing's as if we nev - er said good - bye._____

I don't want to be a - lone, that's all in the

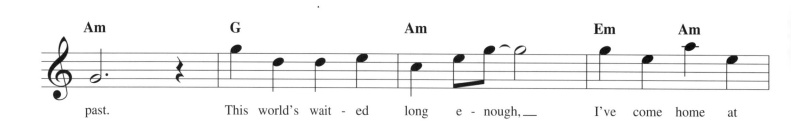

past. This world's wait - ed long e - nough,___ I've come home at

last, and this time will be big - ger,_____ and

bright - er than we knew it._____ So watch me fly,___ we

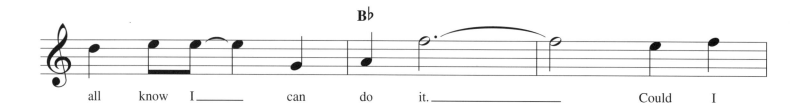

all know I_____ can do it._____ Could I

stop my hand from shak - ing?_____ Has there ev - er been a mo - ment

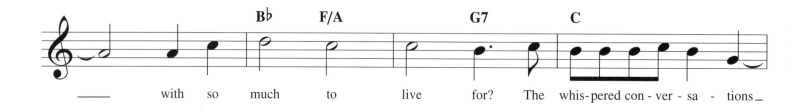

_____ with so much to live for? The whis - pered con - ver - sa - tions_

9

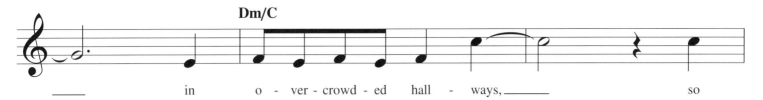

in o - ver - crowd - ed hall - ways,_____ so

much to say, not just to - day,_____ but al - ways._____

_____ We'll have ear - ly morn - ing mad - ness,_____ we'll have

mag - ic in the mak - ing,_____ yes, ev - ery - thing's as if we

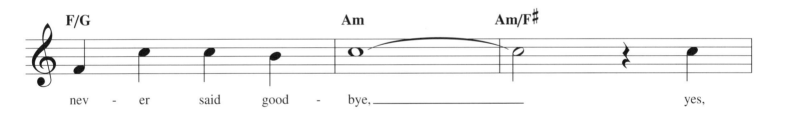

nev - er said good - bye,_____ yes,

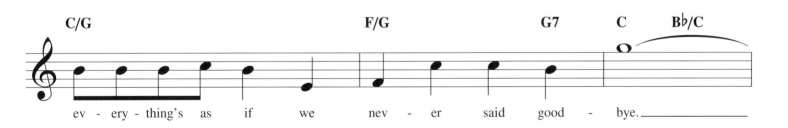

ev - ery - thing's as if we nev - er said good - bye._____

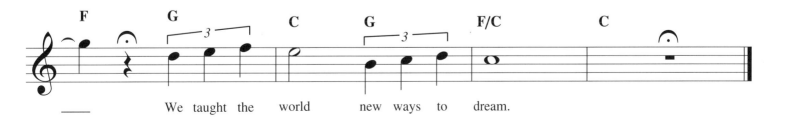

_____ We taught the world new ways to dream.

ALL AT ONCE YOU LOVE HER
from PIPE DREAM

Lyrics by OSCAR HAMMERSTEIN II
Music by RICHARD RODGERS

Slowly

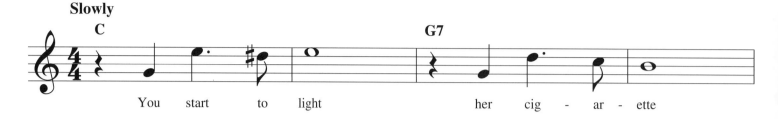

You start to light her cig - ar - ette

and all at once you love her.

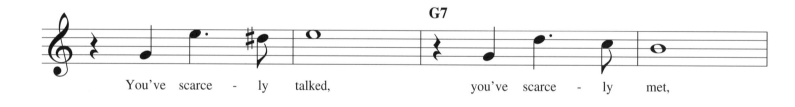

You've scarce - ly talked, you've scarce - ly met,

but all at once you love her.

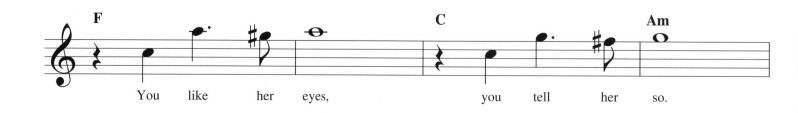

You like her eyes, you tell her so.

She thinks you're wise and clev - er.

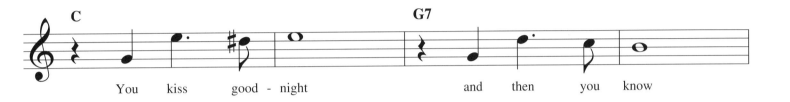

You kiss good - night and then you know

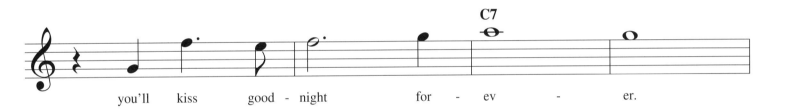

you'll kiss good - night for - ev - er.

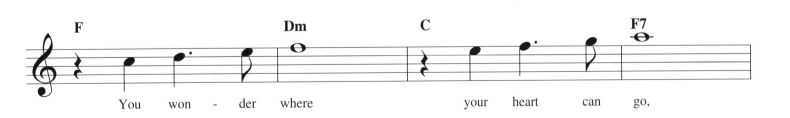

You won - der where your heart can go,

then all at once you know._____

AND ALL THAT JAZZ
from CHICAGO

Words by FRED EBB
Music by JOHN KANDER

Brightly

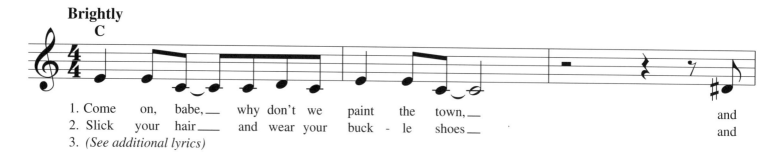

1. Come on, babe,___ why don't we paint the town,___ and
2. Slick your hair___ and wear your buck - le shoes___ and
3. *(See additional lyrics)*

all that jazz!___ I'm gon - na rouge my knees___ and roll my stock - ings down___
all that jazz!___ I hear that Fa - ther Dip___ is gon - na blow the blues___

and all that jazz! Start the car,___ I know a
and all that jazz! Hold on, hon,___ we're gon - na

whoop - ee spot where the gin is cold___ but the pi - an - o's hot. It's just a
bun - ny hug, 'bought some as - pi - rin___ down at U - nit - ed Drug in case we

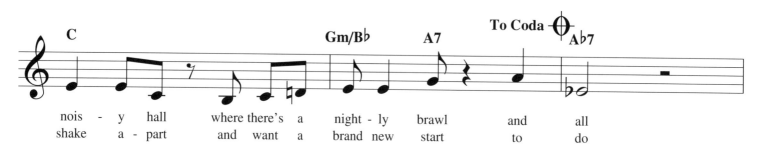

nois - y hall where there's a night - ly brawl and all
shake a - part and want a brand new start to do

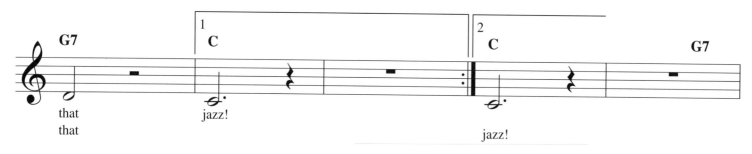

that   that
jazz!   jazz!

Additional Lyrics

3. Find a flask, we're playing fast and loose
   And all that jazz!
   Right up here is where I store the juice
   And all that jazz!

   Come on, babe, we're gonna brush the sky.
   I betcha Lucky Lindy never flew so high,
   'Cause in the stratosphere how could he lend an ear to
   All that jazz!

ANOTHER SUITCASE IN ANOTHER HALL
from EVITA

Words by TIM RICE
Music by ANDREW LLOYD WEBBER

Slowly (8 beat feel)

Eva: I don't ex-pect my love af-fairs _____ to
Time and time a-gain I've said _____ that
Call in three months' time and I'll _____ be

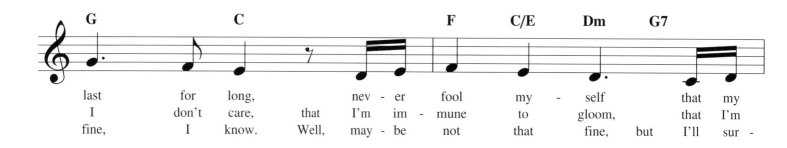

last for long, nev-er fool my-self that my
I don't care, that I'm im-mune to gloom, that I'm
fine, I know. Well, may-be not that fine, but I'll sur-

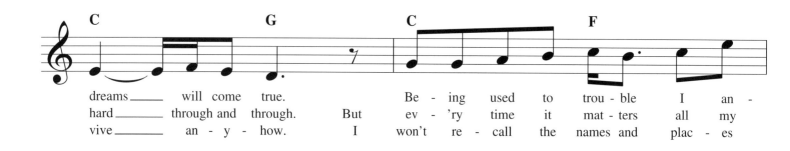

dreams _____ will come true. Be-ing used to trou-ble I an-
hard _____ through and through. But ev-'ry time it mat-ters all my
vive _____ an-y-how. I won't re-call the names and plac-es

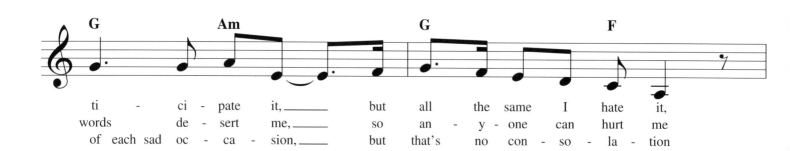

ti-ci-pate it, _____ but all the same I hate it,
words de-sert me, _____ so an-y-one can hurt me
of each sad oc-ca-sion, _____ but that's no con-so-la-tion

would-n't you?
and they do.
here and now.
So what hap-pens now? So what hap-pens

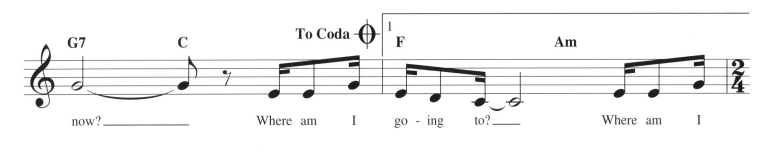

now?_____ Where am I go - ing to?____ Where am I

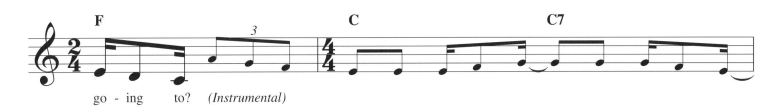

go - ing to? *(Instrumental)*

go - ing to?____ Where am I

go - ing to?____ *(Instrumental)*

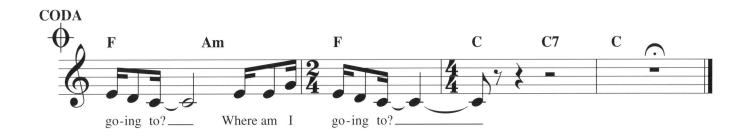

go-ing to?____ Where am I go-ing to?_____

BAUBLES, BANGLES AND BEADS
from KISMET

Words and Music by ROBERT WRIGHT
and GEORGE FORREST
(Music Based on Themes of A. BORODIN)

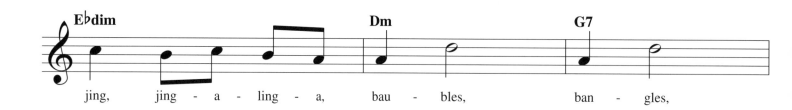

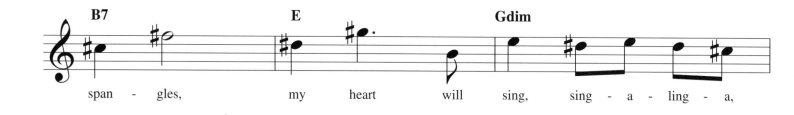

gleam   so,   make

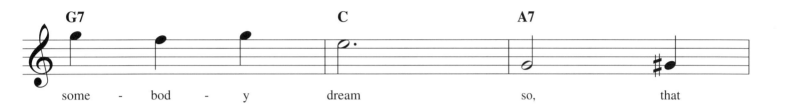

some - bod - y   dream   so,   that

some - day   he   may   buy me   a

ring,   ring - a - ling - a, I've heard   that's where   it

leads,_____ wear - ing bau - bles,

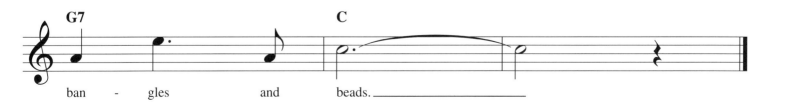

ban - gles and beads._____

THE BEST THINGS IN LIFE ARE FREE
from GOOD NEWS!

Music and Lyrics by B.G. DeSYLVA,
LEW BROWN and RAY HENDERSON

The moon be - longs to

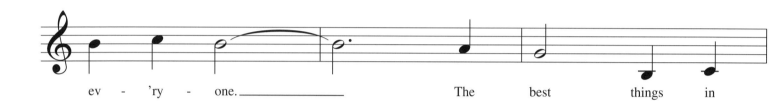

ev - 'ry - one._____ The best things in

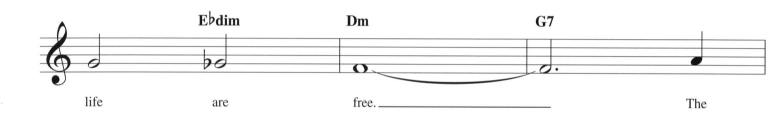

life are free._____ The

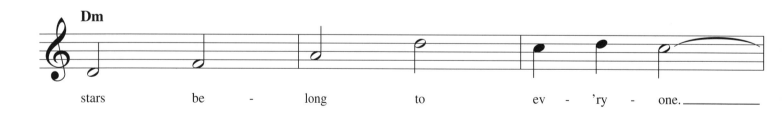

stars be - long to ev - 'ry - one._____

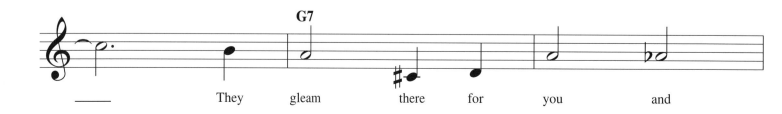

_____ They gleam there for you and

me._____ The flow - ers in Spring, ___

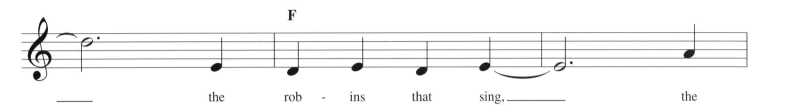

_____ the rob - ins that sing, _____ the

sun - beams that shine, _____ they're yours, they're

mine! And love can come to

ev - 'ry - one. _____ The best things in

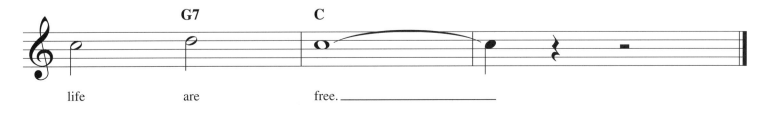

life are free. _____

BIG D
from THE MOST HAPPY FELLA

By FRANK LOESSER

Brightly

You're from Big D ___ I can guess ___ by the way you drawl ___ and the way you dress. ___ You're from Big D, my, oh yes. ___ I mean Big D, lit - tle a, dou - ble l - a - s. ___ And that spells

Dal - las, my dar - lin', dar - lin' Dal - las, don't it
Dal - las, where ev - 'ry home's a pal - ace 'cause the
Dal - las, just dig a toe in Dal - las and there's
Dal - las, I mean it with no mal - ice but the

BIG SPENDER
from SWEET CHARITY

Music by Cy Coleman
Lyrics by Dorothy Fields

Moderately, with a beat

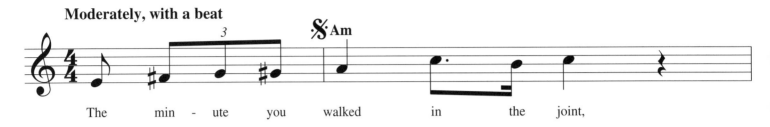

The min - ute you walked in the joint,

I could see you were a man of dis - tinc - tion, a

real big spend - er, ____ good look - ing, ____ so re - fined. ____ Say,

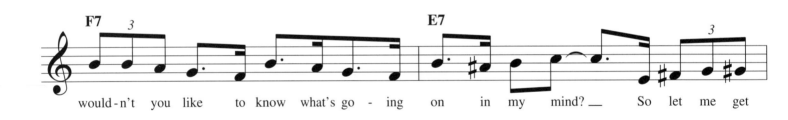

would-n't you like to know what's go - ing on in my mind? ____ So let me get

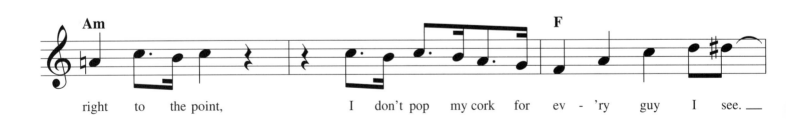

right to the point, I don't pop my cork for ev - 'ry guy I see. ____

____ { Hey! Big spend - er, ____
       { Hey! Big spen - er! ____   spend

a lit - tle time __ with me.

Would - n't you like to have fun, fun, fun? How's a - bout a few

laughs, laughs? I can show you a good time. _____

D.S. al Coda

_____ Let me show you a good time. _____ The min - ute you

CODA

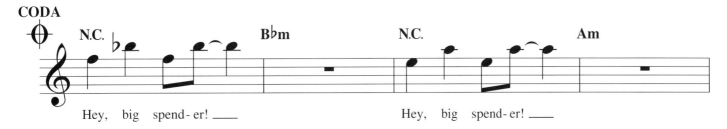

Hey, big spend - er! ___   Hey, big spend - er! ___

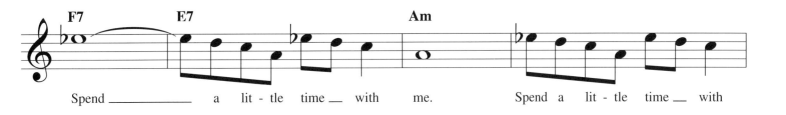

Spend _____ a lit - tle time __ with me.   Spend a lit - tle time __ with

me.   Spend a lit - tle time __ with me. _____

A BUSHEL AND A PECK
from GUYS AND DOLLS

By FRANK LOESSER

Moderately

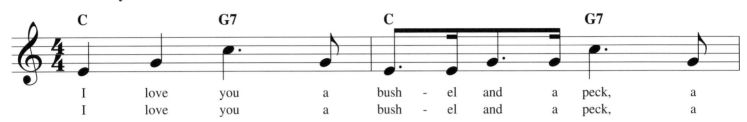

I love you a bush - el and a peck, a
I love you a bush - el and a peck, a

bush - el and a peck and a hug a - round the neck.
bush - el and a peck tho' you make my heart a wreck.

Hug a - round the neck and a bar - rel and a heap,
Make my heart a wreck and you make my life a mess,

bar - rel and a heap and I'm talk - in' in my sleep a - bout
make my life a mess, yes, a mess of hap - pi - ness a - bout

you,_____ a - bout you._____

_____ 'Cause I love you a bush - el and a peck y'

bet your pur - ty neck I do._____

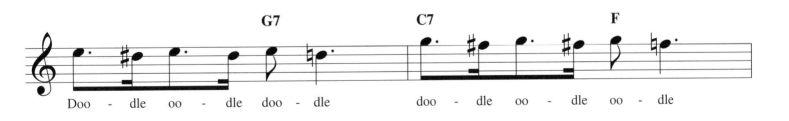

Doo - dle oo - dle doo - dle doo - dle oo - dle oo - dle

doo - dle oo - dle oo - dle ooo._____ _____

BUTTON UP YOUR OVERCOAT
from FOLLOW THRU

Words and Music by B.G. DeSYLVA,
LEW BROWN and RAY HENDERSON

Moderately

But - ton up your o - ver - coat _____
But - ton up your o - ver - coat _____

when the wind is free. Take good _____
when the wind is free. Take good _____

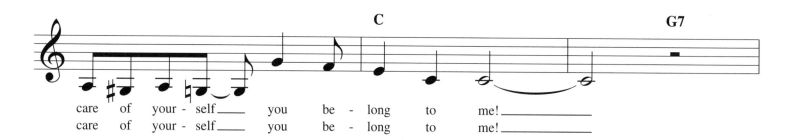

care of your - self _____ you be - long to me! _____
care of your - self _____ you be - long to me! _____

Eat an ap - ple ev - 'ry day; _____ get to bed by
Wear your flan - nel un - der - wear _____ when you climb a

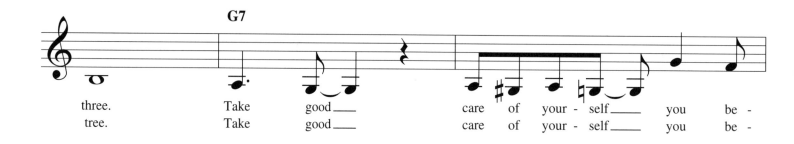

three. Take good _____ care of your - self _____ you be -
tree. Take good _____ care of your - self _____ you be -

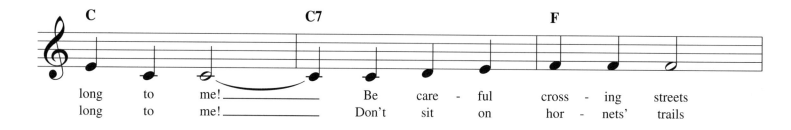

long to me! _____ Be care - ful cross - ing streets
long to me! _____ Don't sit on hor - nets' trails

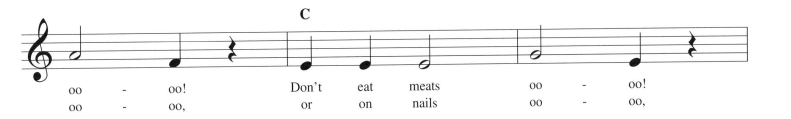

oo - oo!   Don't eat meats   oo - oo!

oo - oo,   or on nails   oo - oo,

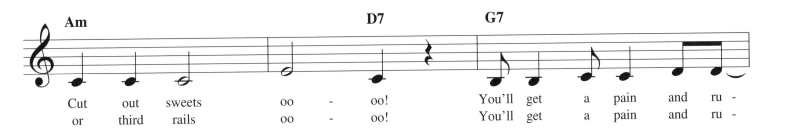

Cut out sweets   oo - oo!   You'll get a pain and ru -

or third rails   oo - oo!   You'll get a pain and ru -

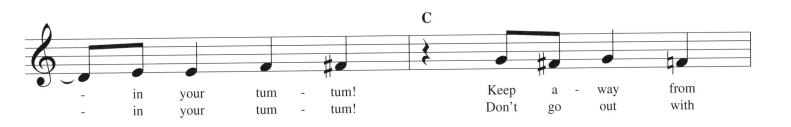

- in your tum - tum!   Keep a - way from

- in your tum - tum!   Don't go out with

boot - leg hootch____   when you're on a spree.

col - lege boys____   when you're on a spree.

Take good____   care of your - self____ you be -

Take good____   care of your - self____ you be -

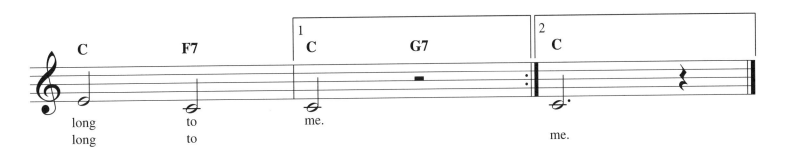

long to me.

long to

CASTLE ON A CLOUD
from LES MISÉRABLES

Music and Lyrics Copyright © 1980 by Editions Musicales Alain Boublil
English Lyrics Copyright © 1986 by Alain Boublil Music Ltd. (ASCAP)
Mechanical and Publication Rights for the U.S.A. Administered by Alain Boublil Music Ltd. (ASCAP)
  c/o Stephen Tenenbaum & Co., Inc., 1775 Broadway, Suite 708, New York, NY 10019,
  Tel. (212) 246-7204, Fax (212) 246-7217

Music by CLAUDE-MICHEL SCHÖNBERG
Lyrics by ALAIN BOUBLIL, JEAN-MARC NATEL
and HERBERT KRETZMER

29

nice to see and she's soft to touch. She

says, "Co - sette, I love you ver - y much."

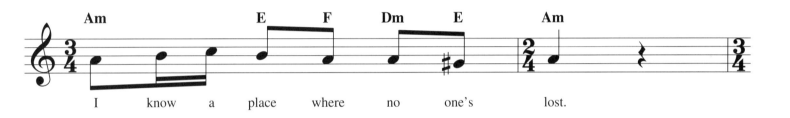

I know a place where no one's lost.

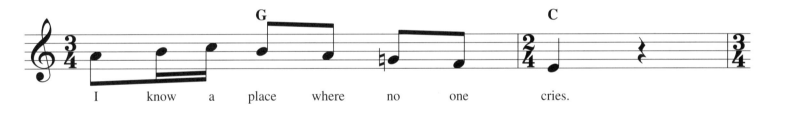

I know a place where no one cries.

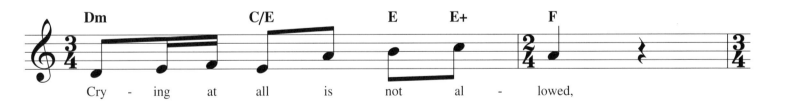

Cry - ing at all is not al - lowed,

not in my cas - tle on a cloud.

CHIM CHIM CHER-EE
from Walt Disney's MARY POPPINS

Words and Music by RICHARD M. SHERMAN
and ROBERT B. SHERMAN

Lightly, with gusto

Chim chim-in-ey, chim chim-in-ey, chim chim cher-ee! A
sweep is as luck-y, as luck-y can be.
Chim chim-in-ey, chim chim-in-ey, chim chim cher-oo! Good
luck will rub off when I shakes 'ands with you, or
blow me a kiss and that's luck-y too. *(Instrumental)*

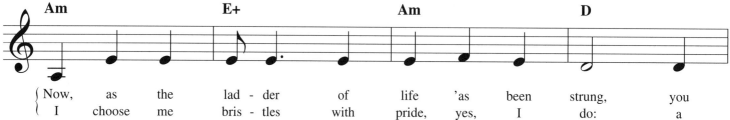

Now, as the lad-der of life 'as been strung, you
I choose me bris-tles with pride, yes, I do: a

'alf - way   in   light.   On   the   roof - tops   of

Lon - don,   coo,   what   a   sight!

Chim chim - in - ey,   chim chim - in - ey,   chim chim cher - ee!   When

you're   with   a   sweep   you're in   glad   com - pa - ny.

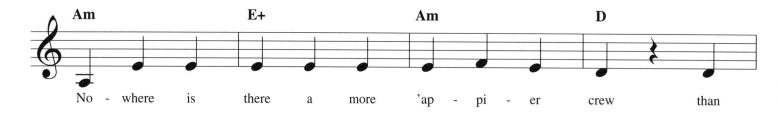

No - where   is   there   a   more   'ap - pi - er   crew   than

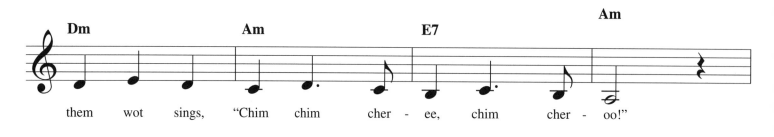

them   wot   sings,   "Chim   chim   cher - ee,   chim   cher - oo!"

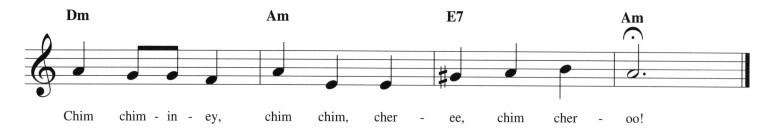

Chim   chim - in - ey,   chim chim,   cher - ee,   chim   cher - oo!

DANCING ON THE CEILING

from SIMPLE SIMON
from EVER GREEN

Words by LORENZ HART
Music by RICHARD RODGERS

Moderately

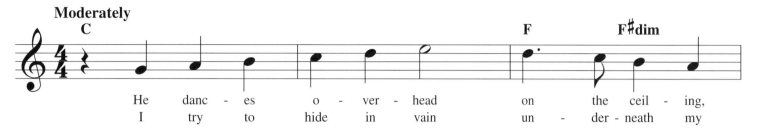

He danc-es o-ver-head on the ceil-ing,
I try to hide in vain un-der-neath my

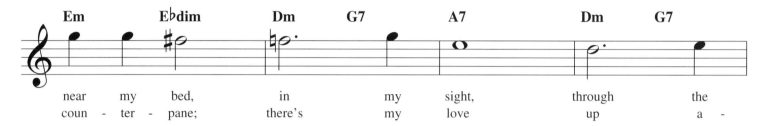

near my bed, in my sight, through the
coun-ter-pane; there's my love up a-

night. I whis-per, "Go a-way, my lov-er,
bove!

it's not fair," but I'm so

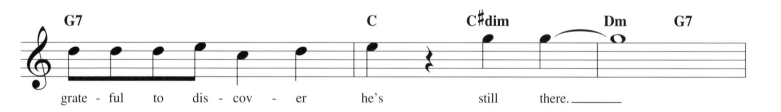

grate-ful to dis-cov-er he's still there.

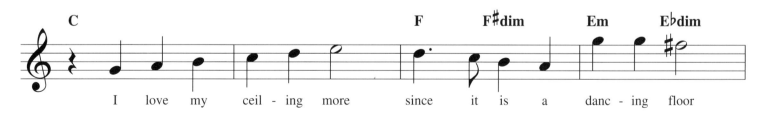

I love my ceil-ing more since it is a danc-ing floor

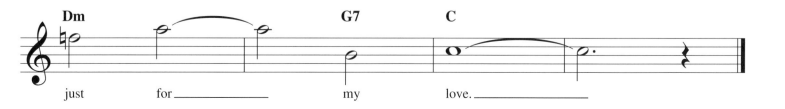

just for my love.

CLOSE AS PAGES IN A BOOK
from UP IN CENTRAL PARK

Words by DOROTHY FIELDS
Music by SIGMUND ROMBERG

Expressively

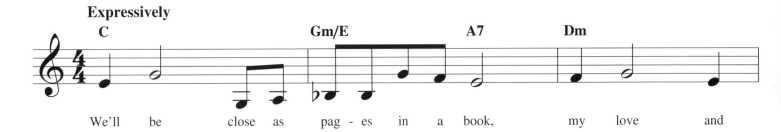

We'll be close as pag - es in a book, my love and

I. So close we can share a sin - gle look,

share ev - 'ry sigh. So close that be -

fore I hear you laugh, my laugh breaks through.

And when a tear starts to ap - pear, my eyes grow mist - y

too. _____ Our dreams won't come tum - bling to the ground,

F D7
we'll hold them fast. Dar - ling, as the
Am D7 G G7 Em
strong - est book is bound, we're 'bout to last. Your life is
E7 Am 3 F G+
my life and while life beats a - way in my heart,
C Gm/E A7 Dm G7
we'll be close as pag - es in a book, nev - er to
1
C G7
2
C B7 Em E7
part. part. Your life is my life and
Am 3 F F7 Em
while life beats a - way in my heart, we'll be close as
A7 Dm G7 C
pag - es in a book, nev - er to part.

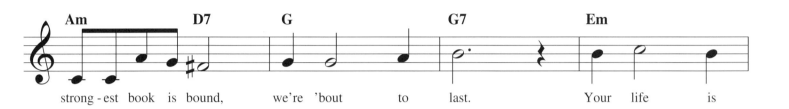

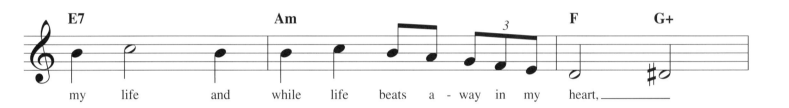

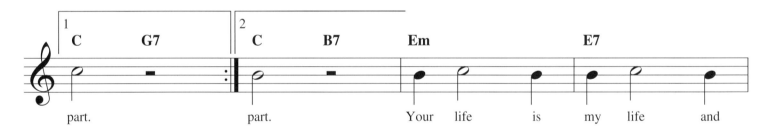

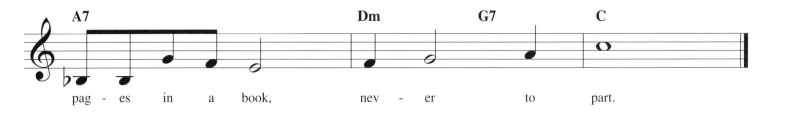

DO I HEAR A WALTZ?
from DO I HEAR A WALTZ?

Music by RICHARD RODGERS
Lyrics by STEPHEN SONDHEIM

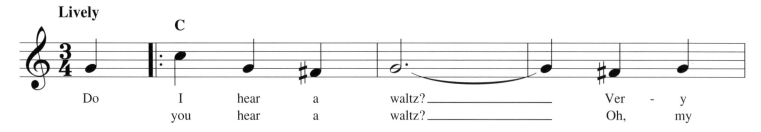

Do I hear a waltz? _____ Ver - y
you hear a waltz? _____ Oh, my

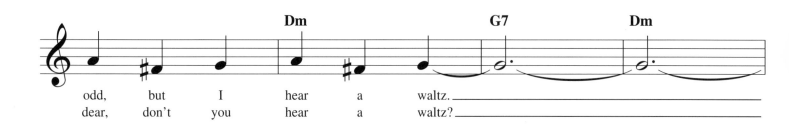

odd, but I hear a waltz. _____
dear, don't you hear a waltz? _____

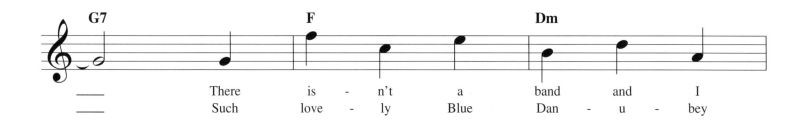

_____ There is - n't a band and I
_____ Such love - ly Blue Dan - u - bey

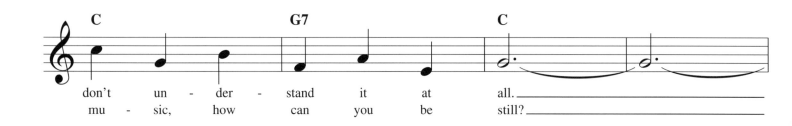

don't un - der - stand it at all. _____
mu - sic, how can you be still? _____

_____ I can hear a waltz. _____
_____ You must hear a waltz! _____

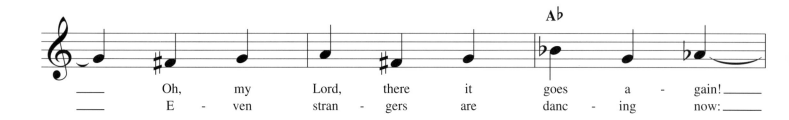

_____ Oh, my Lord, there it goes a - gain! _____
_____ E - ven stran - gers are danc - ing now: _____

Why   is   no - bod - y   danc - ing____
An   old   la - dy   is   waltz - ing____

____   in   the   street?_____   Can't   they____
____   in   her   flat,_____   waltz - ing____

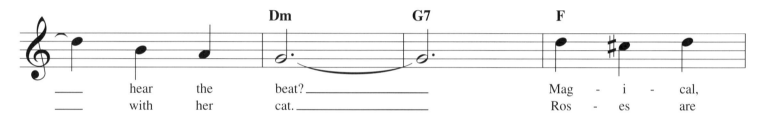

____   hear   the   beat?_____   Mag - i - cal,
____   with   her   cat._____   Ros - es   are

mys - ti - cal,   mir - a - cle,_____   can   it
danc - ing   with   pe - o - nies,_____   yes,   it's

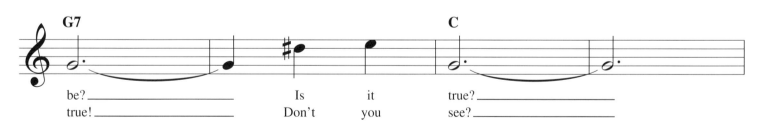

be?_____   Is   it   true?_____
true!_____   Don't   you   see?_____

Things   are   im - pos - si - bly   lyr - i - cal._____
Ev - 'ry - thing's   sud - den - ly   Vi - en - nese._____

DON'T CRY OUT LOUD

(We Don't Cry Out Loud)

from THE BOY FROM OZ

Words and Music by PETER ALLEN
and CAROLE BAYER SAGER

Slowly

Ba - by cried the day the cir - cus came_____ to
Ba - by saw that when they pulled_____ the big_____ top

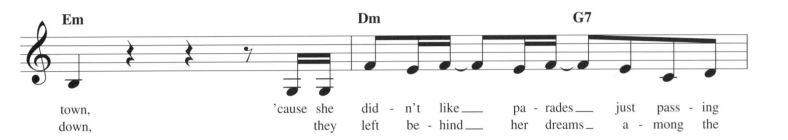

town, 'cause she did - n't like_____ pa - rades_____ just pass - ing
down, they left be - hind_____ her dreams_ a - mong the

by her. So she paint - ed on a smile and took up with_____ some
lit - ter. And the dif - f'rent kind of love she thought_ she'd

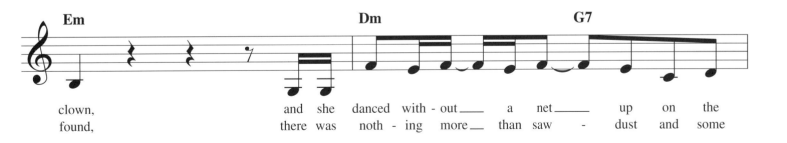

clown, and she danced with - out_____ a net_____ up on the
found, there was noth - ing more_____ than saw - dust and some

wire._____ I know a lot_____ a - bout_____ her 'cause you
glit - ter. But ba - by can't_____ be bro - ken 'cause you

see;   ba - by is____ an aw - ful lot like
see,   she had the fin - est teach - er, that was

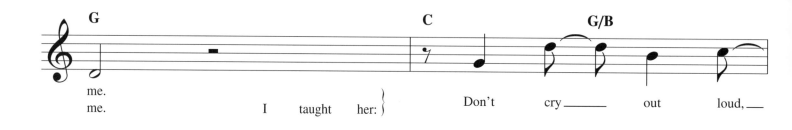

me.   I taught her: Don't   cry____ out   loud,__
me.

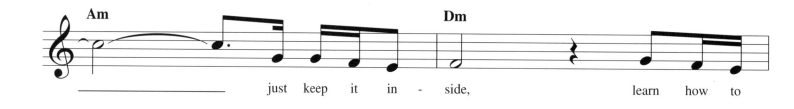

_____ just keep it in - side,   learn how to

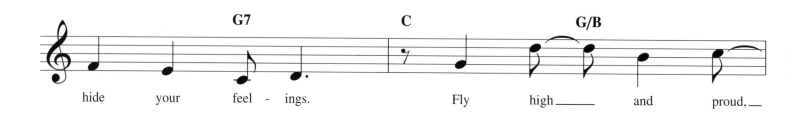

hide   your   feel - ings.   Fly   high____ and   proud,__

_____ and if you should fall,   re - mem - ber you

al - most had it all._____

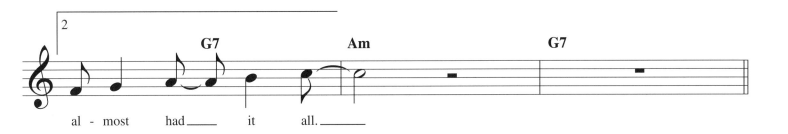

al - most had____ it all._____

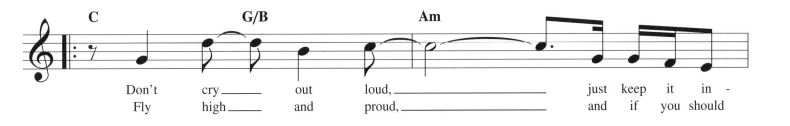

Don't cry_____ out loud,_____ just keep it in -
Fly high_____ and proud,_____ and if you should

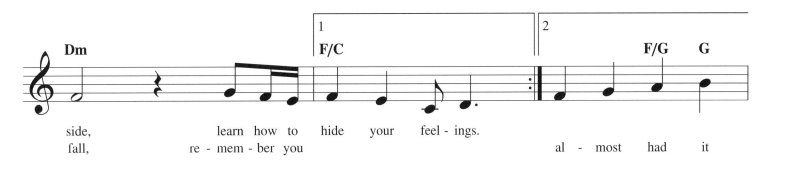

side,   learn how to hide your feel - ings.
fall,   re - mem - ber you   al - most had it

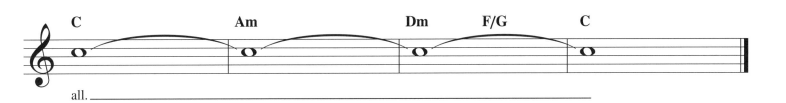

all._____

EVERYBODY'S GOT A HOME BUT ME
from PIPE DREAM

Lyrics by OSCAR HAMMERSTEIN II
Music by RICHARD RODGERS

Slowly, with expression

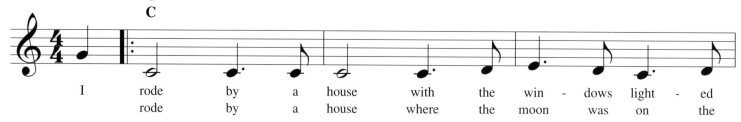

I rode by a house with the win - dows light - ed
rode by a house where the moon was on the

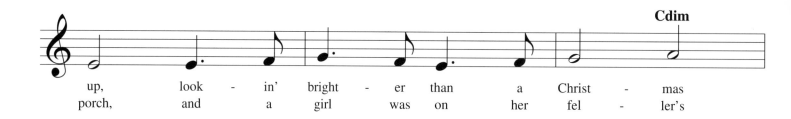

up, look - in' bright - er than a Christ - mas
porch, and a girl was on her fel - ler's

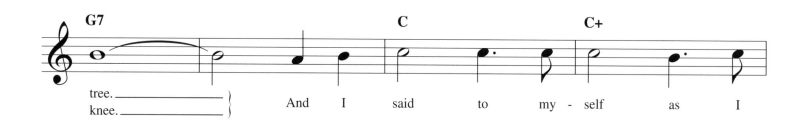

tree. And I said to my - self as I
knee.

rode by my - self, ev - 'ry - bod - y's got a

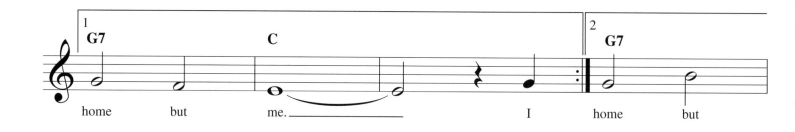

home but me. I
home but

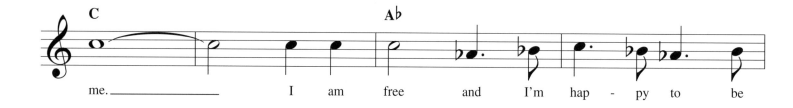

me. I am free and I'm hap - py to be

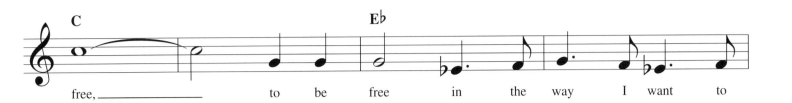

free, _____ to be free in the way I want to

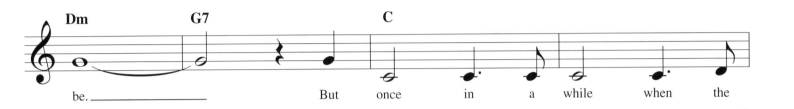

be. _____ But once in a while when the

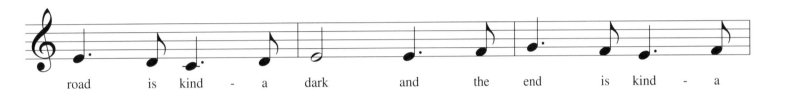

road is kind - a dark and the end is kind - a

hard to see, _____ I look up and I

cry to a cloud go - in' by: "Won't there

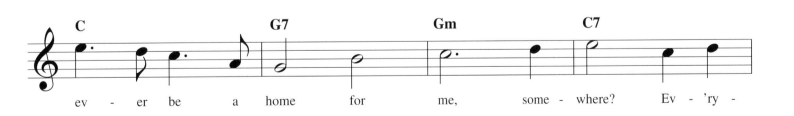

ev - er be a home for me, some - where? Ev - 'ry -

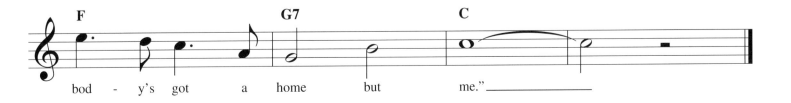

bod - y's got a home but me." _____

FIDDLER ON THE ROOF
from the Musical FIDDLER ON THE ROOF

Words by SHELDON HARNICK
Music by JERRY BOCK

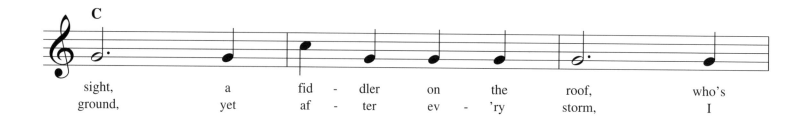

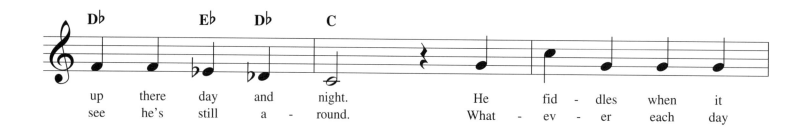

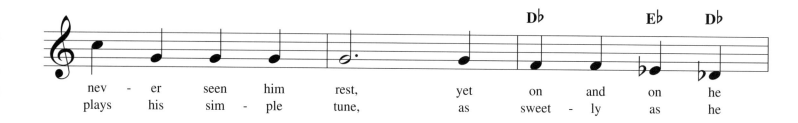

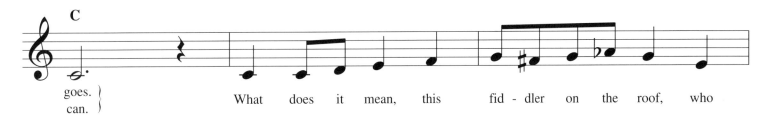

goes.
can.
What does it mean, this fid - dler on the roof, who

fid - dles ev - 'ry night and fid - dles ev - 'ry noon? Why should he pick so

cu - ri - ous a place to play his lit - tle fid - dler's tune? An

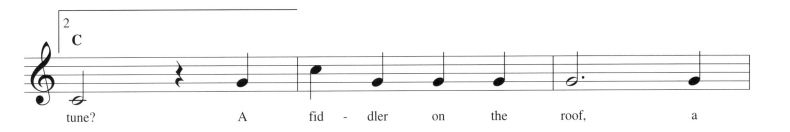

tune? A fid - dler on the roof, a

most un - like - ly sight, it might not mean a

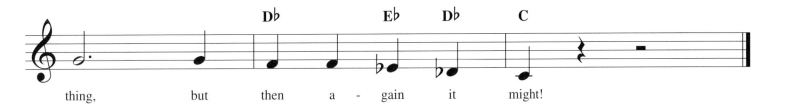

thing, but then a - gain it might!

FIND YOUR GRAIL
from MONTY PYTHON'S SPAMALOT

Lyrics by ERIC IDLE
Music by JOHN DU PREZ and ERIC IDLE

International Pop Ballad

LADY OF THE LAKE:

If you trust in your soul, keep your eyes on the
strong. Keep right on to the end of your
right to the end. You'll find your goal, my

goal. Then the prize you won't fail. That's your Grail. That's your
song. Do not fail. Find your Grail. Find your Grail Find your
friend. You won't fail. Find your Grail. Find your Grail. Find your

1.
Grail. So, be

2.
Grail. Life is real - ly

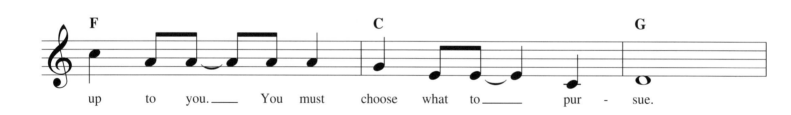

up to you.___ You must choose what to ___ pur - sue.

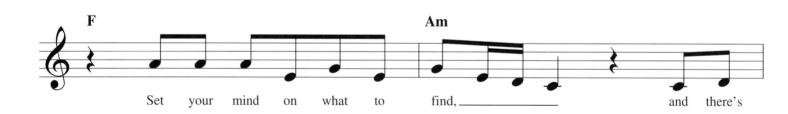

Set your mind on what to find, ___ and there's

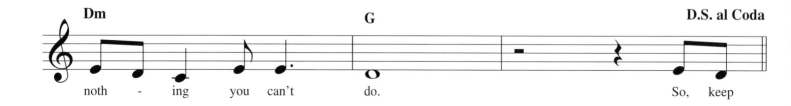

noth - ing you can't do. So, keep

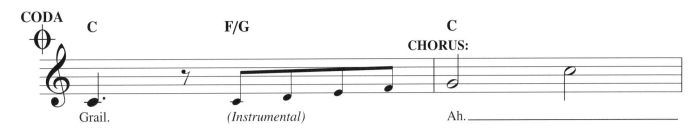

CODA

C   **F/G**   **C**
CHORUS:

Grail.   *(Instrumental)*   Ah. _____

G   **Am**   **Am/G**   **F**

_____   Ah. _____

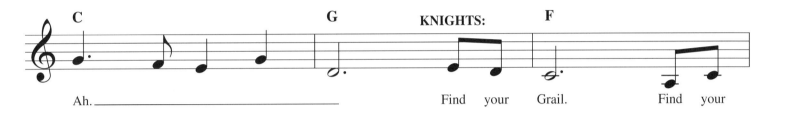

C   **G**   **KNIGHTS:**   **F**

Ah. _____   Find your Grail.   Find your

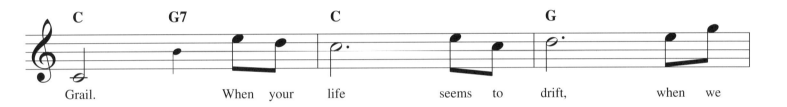

C   **G7**   **C**   **G**

Grail.   When your life   seems to drift,   when we

Am   **Am/G**   **F**   **C**   **C/E**

all   need a   lift,   trim your sail.   You won't

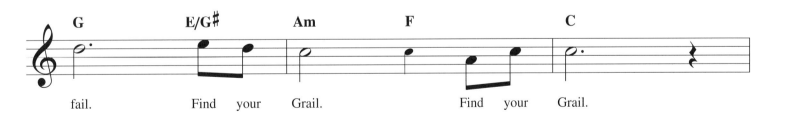

G   **E/G♯**   **Am**   **F**   **C**

fail.   Find your Grail.   Find your Grail.

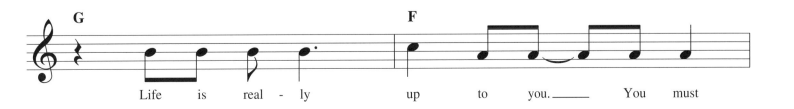

G   **F**

Life is real - ly   up to you. _____ You must

48

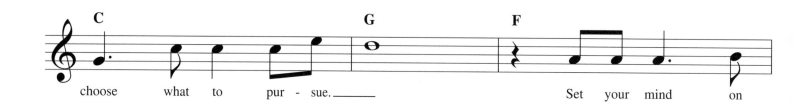

choose what to pur - sue.＿＿＿ Set your mind on

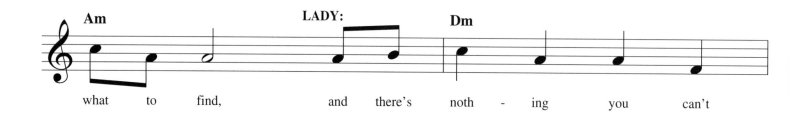

what to find, and there's noth - ing you can't

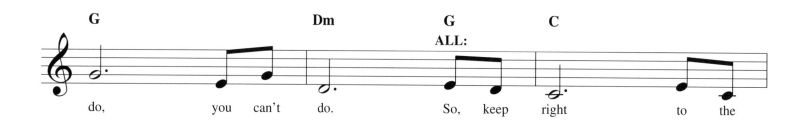

do, you can't do. So, keep right to the

end. You'll find your goal, my

friend. Find your Grail. You won't fail. Find your

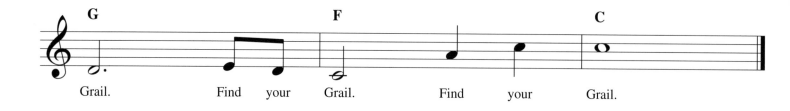

Grail. Find your Grail. Find your Grail.

GONNA BUILD A MOUNTAIN
from the Musical Production STOP THE WORLD – I WANT TO GET OFF

Words and Music by LESLIE BRICUSSE
and ANTHONY NEWLEY

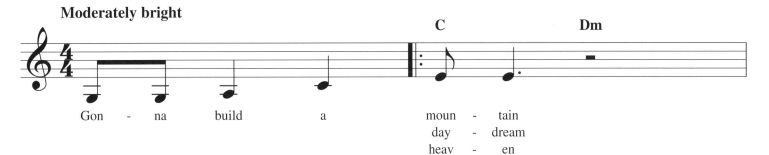

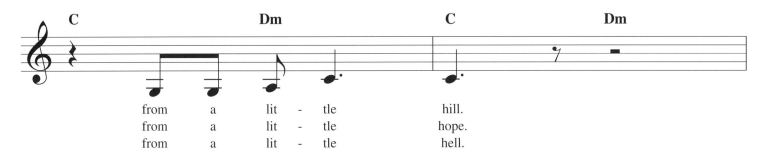

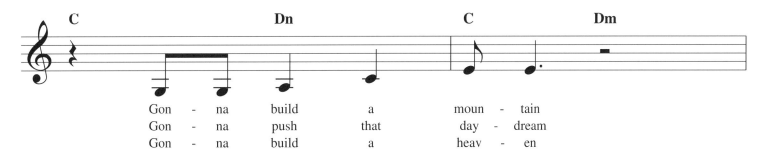

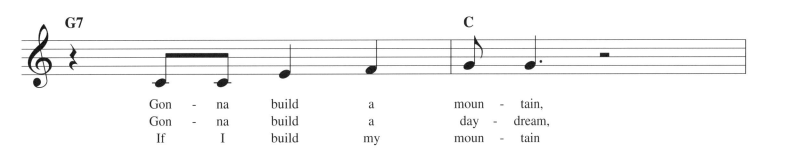

51

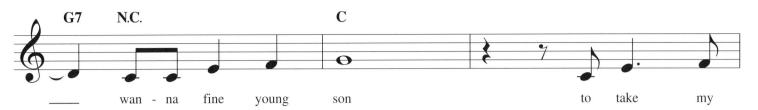

wan - na fine young son to take my

place. I'll leave a son in my heav - en on

earth, with the Lord's good grace.

With a fine young son

to take my place,

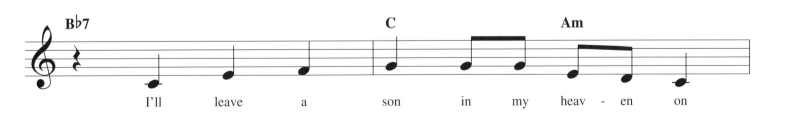

I'll leave a son in my heav - en on

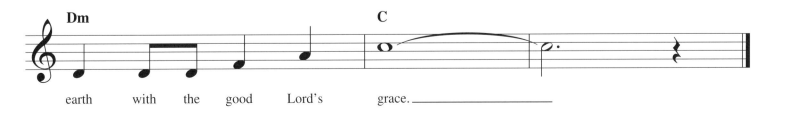

earth with the good Lord's grace.

FROM THIS MOMENT ON

from OUT OF THIS WORLD
from FOSSE

Words and Music by
COLE PORTER

Fast tempo

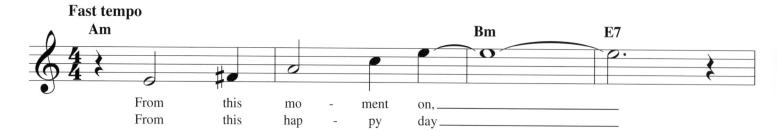

From this mo - ment on,
From this hap - py day

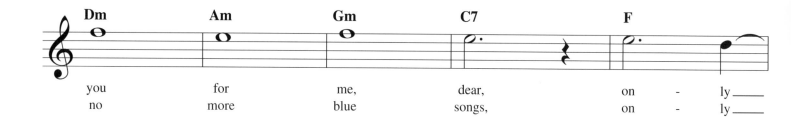

you for me, dear, on - ly
no more blue songs, on - ly

two for tea, dear, from this
whoop - dee - doo songs, from this

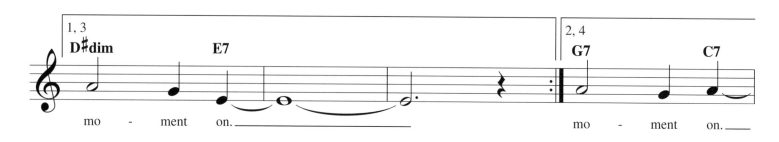

1, 3
mo - ment on.

2, 4
mo - ment on.

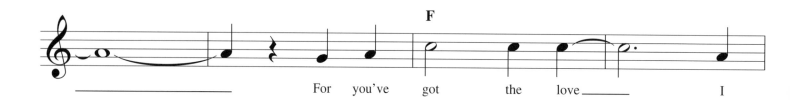

For you've got the love I

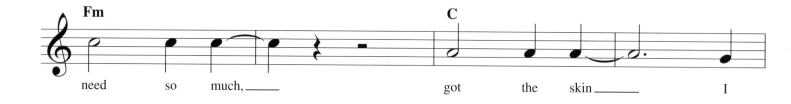

need so much, got the skin I

THE GIRL THAT I MARRY
from the Stage Production ANNIE GET YOUR GUN

Words and Music by
IRVING BERLIN

Moderately

The girl that I mar - ry will

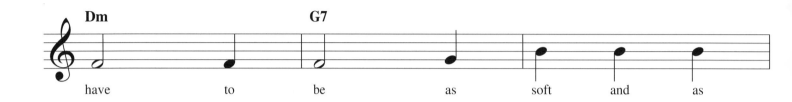

have to be as soft and as

pink as a nurs - er - y. The

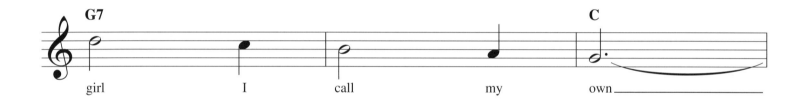

girl I call my own_____

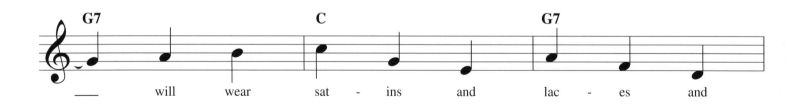

___ will wear sat - ins and lac - es and

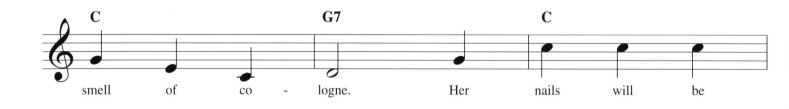

smell of co - logne. Her nails will be

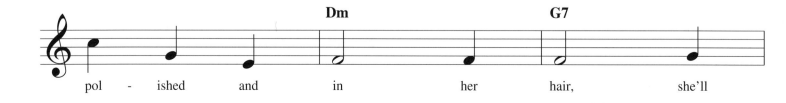

pol - ished and in her hair, she'll

wear a gar - de - nia and I'll be

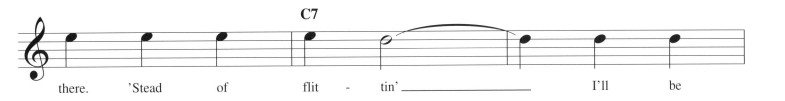

there. 'Stead of flit - tin' _____ I'll be

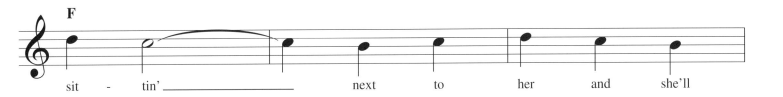

sit - tin' _____ next to her and she'll

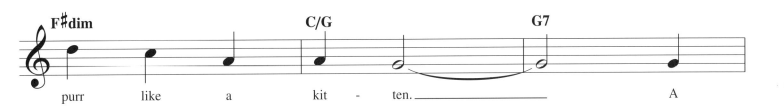

purr like a kit - ten. _____ A

doll I can car - ry, the girl that I

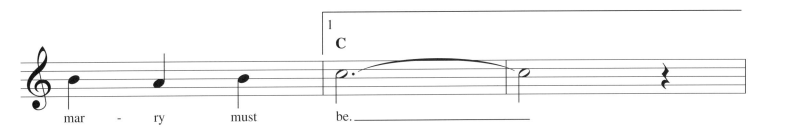

mar - ry must be. _____

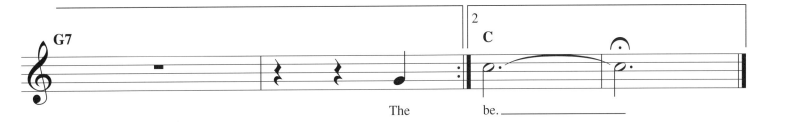

The be. _____

GLAD TO BE UNHAPPY
from ON YOUR TOES

Words by LORENZ HART
Music by RICHARD RODGERS

Reflectively

Fools rush in, so here I am

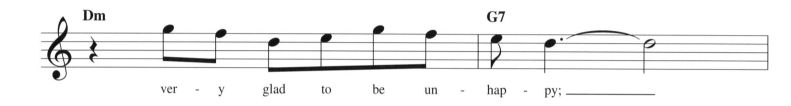

ver - y glad to be un - hap - py;

I can't win, but here I am,

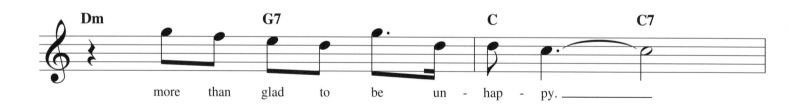

more than glad to be un - hap - py.

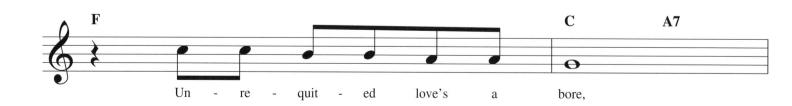

Un - re - quit - ed love's a bore,

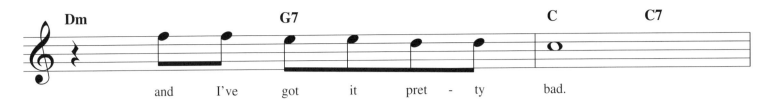

and I've got it pret - ty bad.

But for some - one you a - dore,

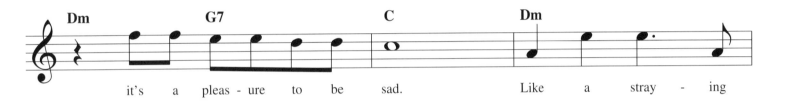

it's a pleas - ure to be sad. Like a stray - ing

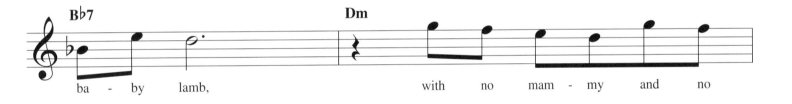

ba - by lamb, with no mam - my and no

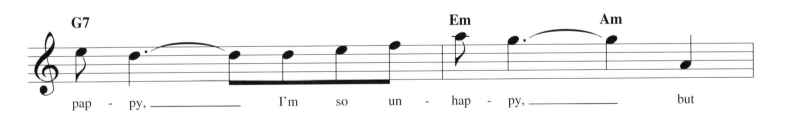

pap - py, _____ I'm so un - hap - py, _____ but

oh, so glad!

HAVE YOU MET MISS JONES?
from I'D RATHER BE RIGHT

Words by LORENZ HART
Music by RICHARD RODGERS

Medium Swing

"Have you met Miss Jones?" Some - one said as

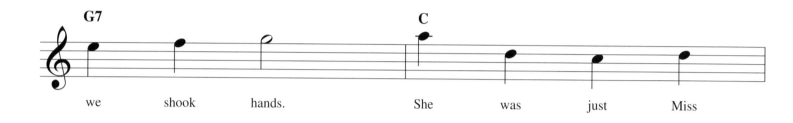

we shook hands. She was just Miss

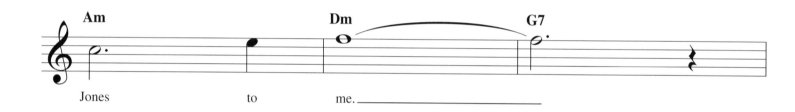

Jones to me.

Then I said, "Miss Jones, You're a girl who

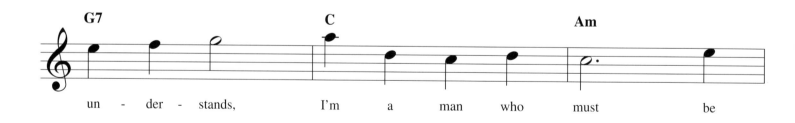

un - der - stands, I'm a man who must be

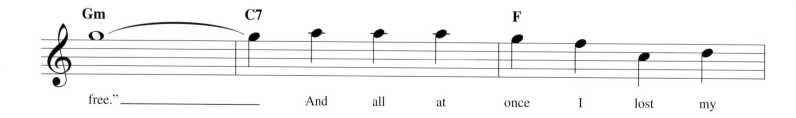

free." And all at once I lost my

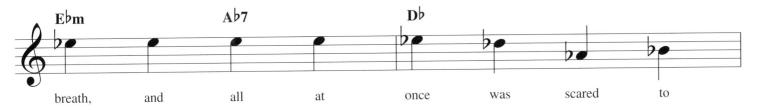

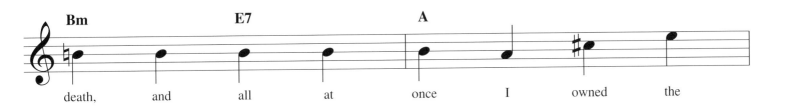

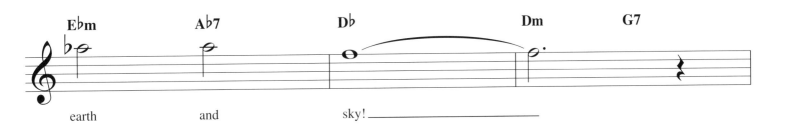

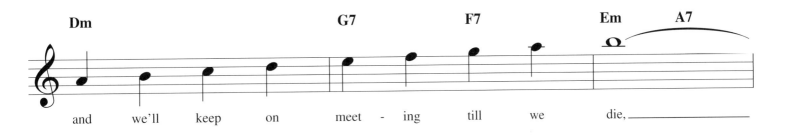

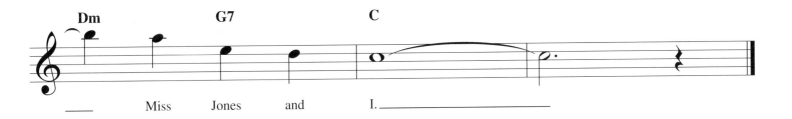

HEY, LOOK ME OVER
from WILDCAT

Music by CY COLEMAN
Lyrics by CAROLYN LEIGH

March tempo

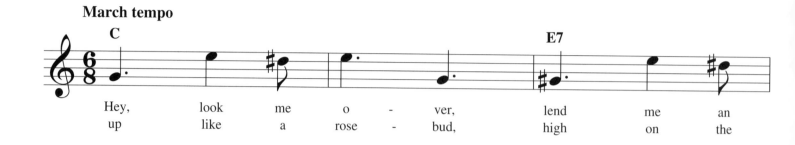

Hey, look me o - ver, lend me an
up like a rose - bud, high on the

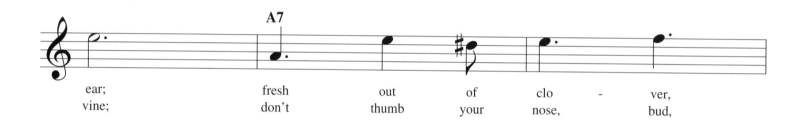

ear; fresh out of clo - ver,
vine; don't thumb of your nose, bud,

mort - gaged up to here. But don't pass the
take a tip from

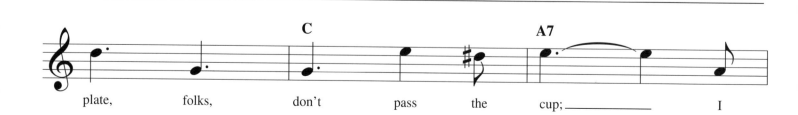

plate, folks, don't pass the cup; I

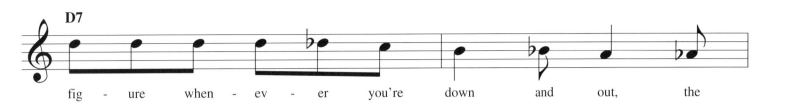

fig - ure when - ev - er you're down and out, the

on - ly way is up. And I'll be mine. I'm a

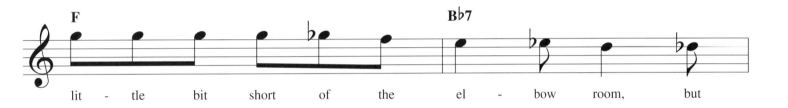

lit - tle bit short of the el - bow room, but

let me get me some, { And look out, / Hear me shout, } world,

here I come.

I BELIEVE MY HEART
from THE WOMAN IN WHITE

Music by ANDREW LLOYD WEBBER
Lyrics by DAVID ZIPPEL

Moderately

HARTRIGHT: When - ev - er I look at you,_____
LAURA: The life - time be - fore we met_____

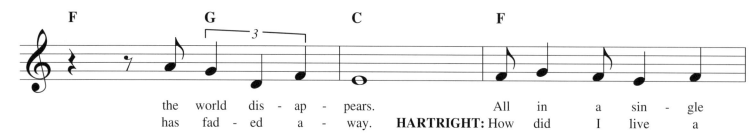

the world dis - ap - pears. All in a sin - gle
has fad - ed a - way. **HARTRIGHT:** How did I live a

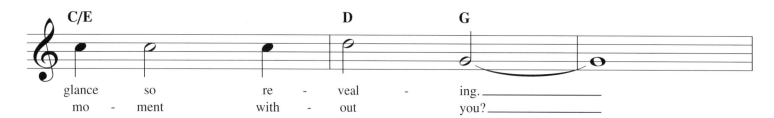

glance so re - veal - ing._____
mo - ment with - out you?_____

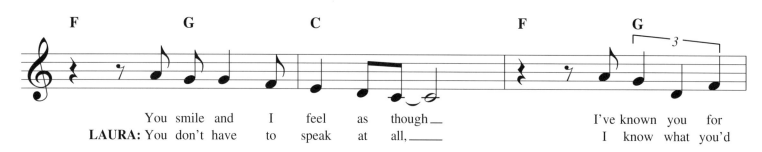

You smile and I feel as though_____ I've known you for
LAURA: You don't have to speak at all,_____ I know what you'd

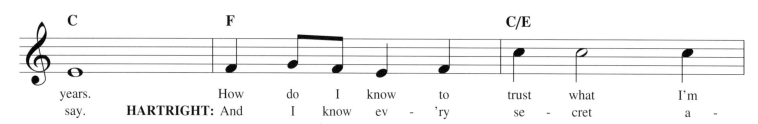

years. How do I know to trust what I'm
say. **HARTRIGHT:** And I know ev - 'ry se - cret a -

feel - ing?_____ **LAURA:** I be - lieve my
bout you._____ I be - lieve my

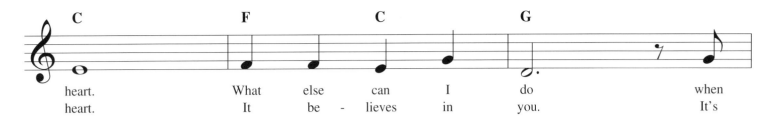

heart.   What else can I do when
heart.   It be - lieves in you. It's

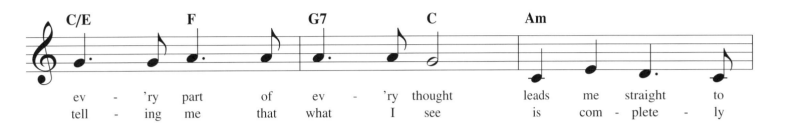

ev - 'ry part of ev - 'ry thought leads me straight to
tell - ing me that what I see is com - plete - ly

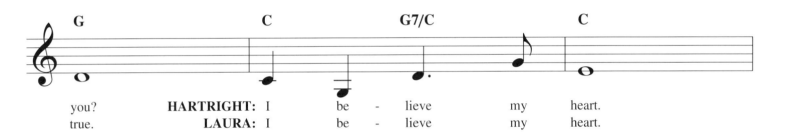

you?   **HARTRIGHT:** I be - lieve my heart.
true.   **LAURA:** I be - lieve my heart.

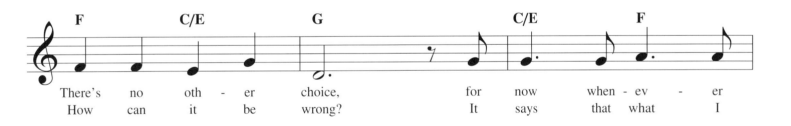

There's no oth - er choice, for now when - ev - er
How can it be wrong? It says that what I

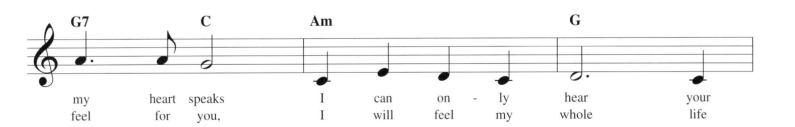

my heart speaks I can on - ly hear your
feel for you, I will feel my whole life

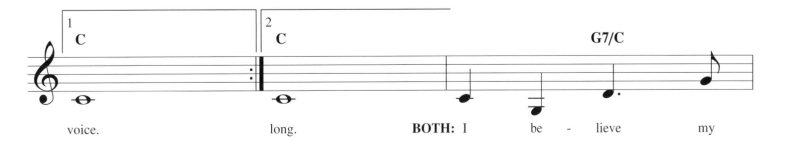

voice. long.   **BOTH:** I be - lieve my

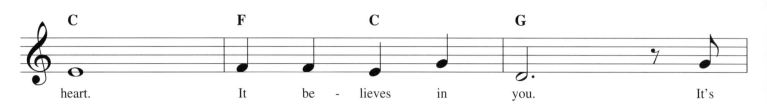

heart. It be - lieves in you. It's

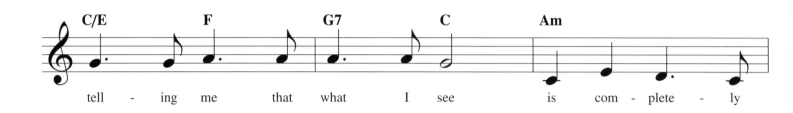

tell - ing me that what I see is com - plete - ly

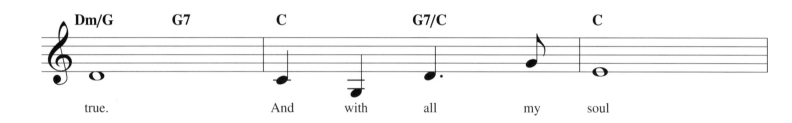

true. And with all my soul

I be - lieve my heart. The

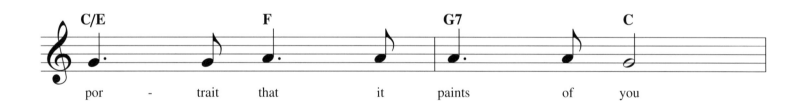

por - trait that it paints of you

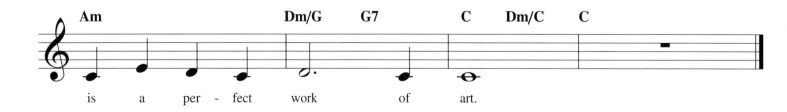

is a per - fect work of art.

I DON'T KNOW HOW TO LOVE HIM
from JESUS CHRIST SUPERSTAR

Words by TIM RICE
Music by ANDREW LLOYD WEBBER

Slowly, tenderly and very expressively

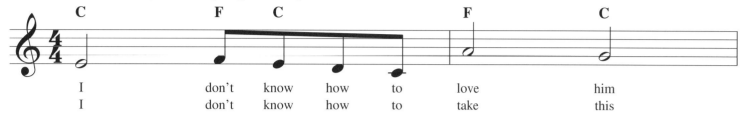

I don't know how to love him
I don't know how to take this

what to do how to move him. I've been
I don't see why he moves me. He's a

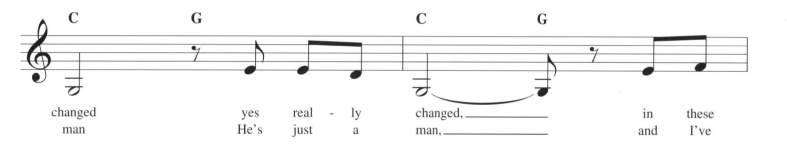

changed yes real - ly changed, in these
man He's just a man, and I've

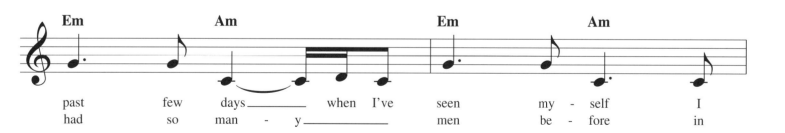

past few days when I've seen my - self I
had so man - y men be - fore in

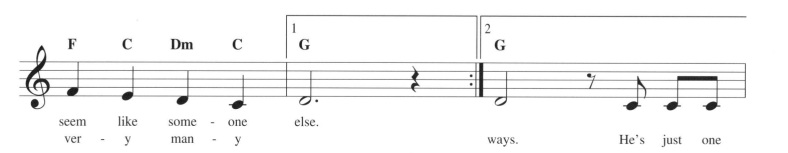

seem like some - one else.
ver - y man - y

ways. He's just one

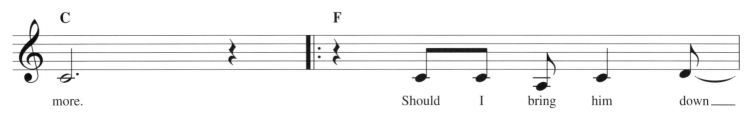

more.　　　Should I bring him down＿＿

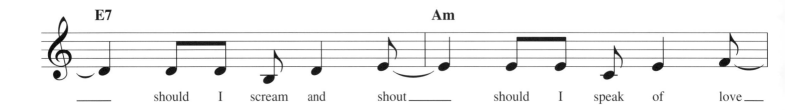

＿＿ should I scream and shout＿＿ should I speak of love＿＿

＿＿ let my feel - ings out?＿＿＿ I nev - er thought I'd

come to this＿＿＿ what's it all a -

bout?＿＿＿＿＿＿＿＿ { Don't you think it's rath - er
　　　　　　　　　　　　　　　　　　 { Yet if he said he

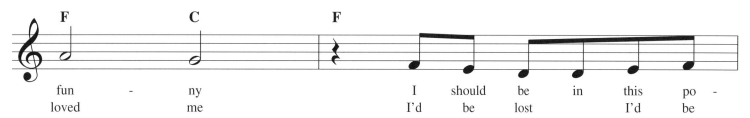

fun - ny   I should be in this po-
loved me   I'd be lost   I'd be

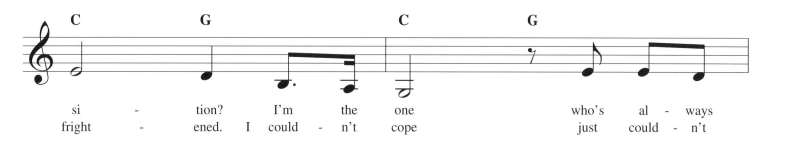

si - tion? I'm the one   who's al-ways
fright - ened. I could-n't cope   just could-n't

been   so calm so cool,
cope   I'd turn my head

no lov-er's fool   run - ning ev-'ry
I'd back a-way I would-n't want to

show,   He scares me so.
know,   He scares me

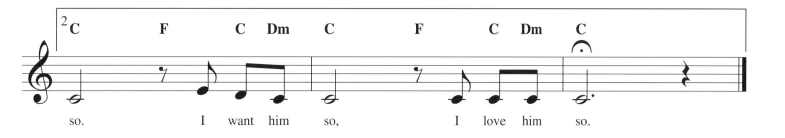

so.   I want him so,   I love him so.

I CAIN'T SAY NO
from OKLAHOMA!

Lyrics by OSCAR HAMMERSTEIN II
Music by RICHARD RODGERS

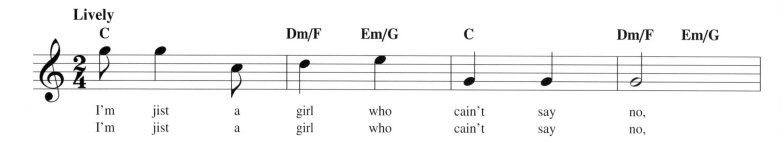

Lively

I'm jist a girl who cain't say no,
I'm jist a girl who cain't say no,

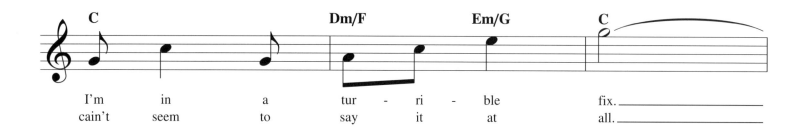

I'm in a tur-ri-ble fix.
cain't seem to say it at all.

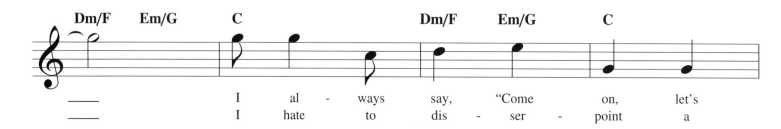

I al-ways say, "Come on, let's
I hate to dis-ser-point a

go," jist when I ort-a say
beau when he is pay-in' a

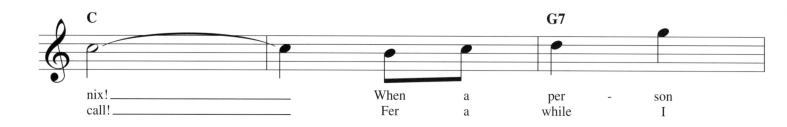

nix! When a per-son
call! Fer a while I

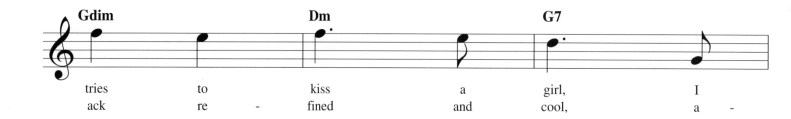

tries to kiss a girl, I
ack re-fined and cool, a-

69

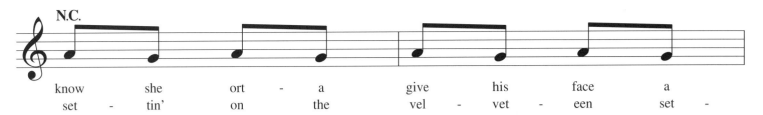

know she ort - a give his face a
set - tin' on the vel - vet - een set -

C   G7
smack, _____ but as soon as
ee, _____ nen I think of

Gdim   Dm   G7
some - one kiss - es me,   I
thet ol' gold - en rule,   and

N.C.
some - how, sort - a, want - a kiss him
do fer him what he would do him fer

                              C
back! _____ I'm jist a
me! _____ I cain't re -

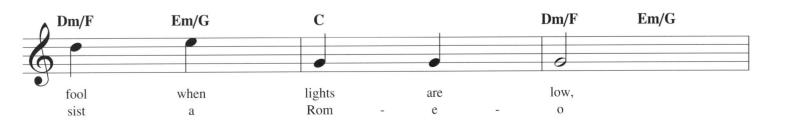

Dm/F   Em/G   C   Dm/F   Em/G
fool when lights are low,
sist a Rom - e - o

I cain't be priss - y and quaint, _____
in a som - brer - o and chaps. _____

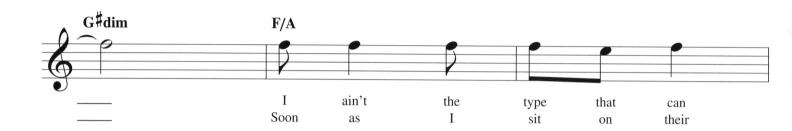

_____ I ain't the type that can
_____ Soon as I sit on their

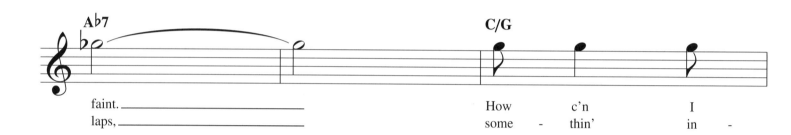

faint. _____ How c'n I
laps, _____ some - thin' in -

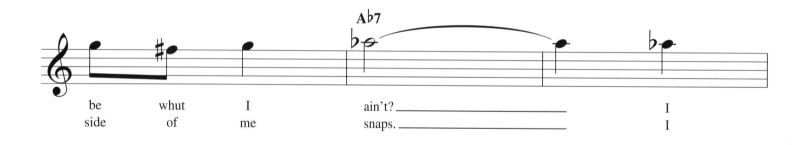

be whut I ain't? _____ I
side of me snaps. _____ I

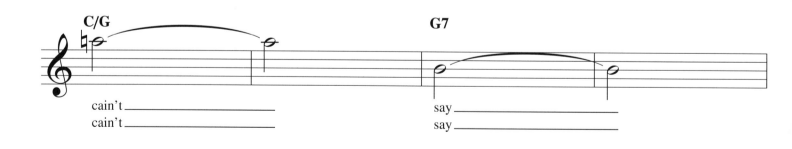

cain't _____ say _____
cain't _____ say _____

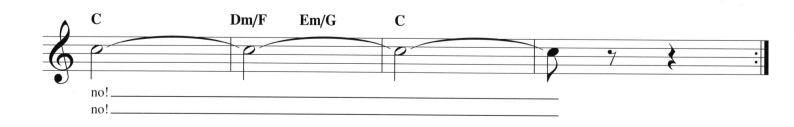

no! _____
no! _____

I GO TO RIO
from THE BOY FROM OZ

Words and Music by PETER ALLEN
and ADRIENNE ANDERSON

With a Latin beat

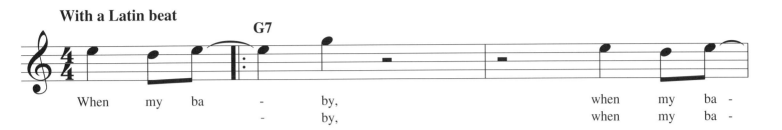

When my ba - by,   when my ba -
    - by,   when my ba -

- by smiles at me   I go to Ri -
- by smiles at me   I feel like Tar -

- o   de Ja - nei - ro.
- zan   of the Jun - gle.

My oh me   oh,   I go wild
There on the hot   sand   and in a bun -

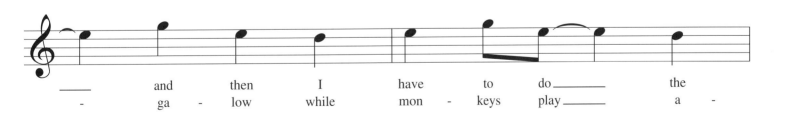

and then I have to do   the
- ga - low while mon - keys play   a -

Sam - ba   and La Bam - ba.
bove - a   we'll make love - a.

Now I'm not the kind_____ of per -
Now I'm not the type_____ to let_____

- son with a pas - sion - ate_____ per -
_____ vi - bra - tions trig - ger my_____ i -

sua - sion for danc - in'_____ or ro -
mag - i - na - tion eas - i - ly._____ You know that's

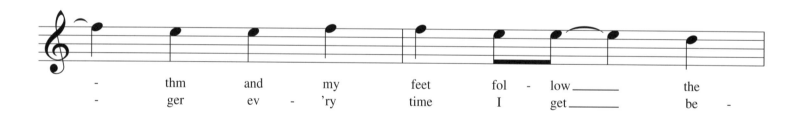

manc - in'. But I give in to the rhy -
just not me. But I turn in - to a ti -

- thm and my feet fol - low_____ the
- ger ev - 'ry time I get_____ be -

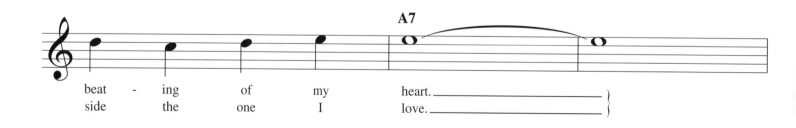

beat - ing of my heart._____
side the one I love._____

Whoa,_____ when my ba - by,_____

when my ba - by smiles at me I go to

C

Ri - o de Ja - nei - ro.

G7

I'm a Sal - sa fel - low. When my ba -

Dm/B

- by smiles at me the sun lights

E7 **Am** **D7**

up my life and I feel free at last,

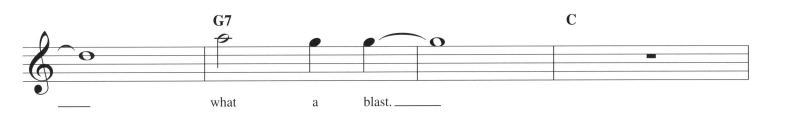

G7 **C**

what a blast.

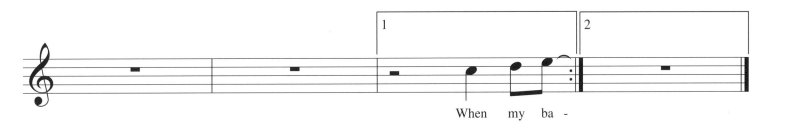

1 2

When my ba -

I LOVE PARIS
from CAN-CAN
from HIGH SOCIETY

Words and Music by
COLE PORTER

Moderately

I love Par - is in the spring - time, _____

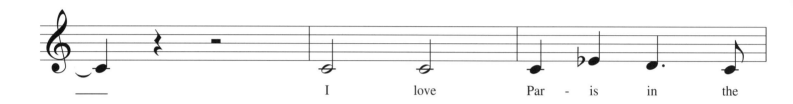

_____ I love Par - is in the

fall, _____ I love

Par - is in the win - ter, when it driz - zles,

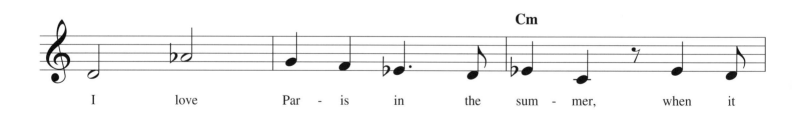

I love Par - is in the sum - mer, when it

siz - zles. I Love Par - is ev - 'ry

mo - ment, _____ ev - 'ry

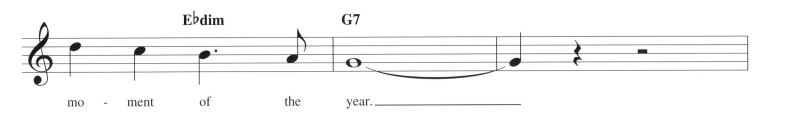

mo - ment of the year. _____

I love Par - is, why, oh why, do

I love Par - is? Be - cause my love is

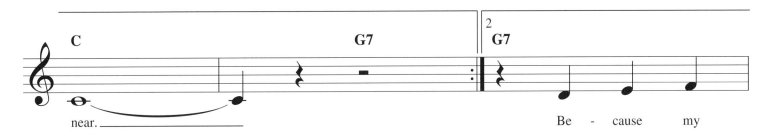

near. _____ Be - cause my

love, _____ be - cause my love _____

____ is near. _____

I WILL NEVER LEAVE YOU
from SIDE SHOW

Words by BILL RUSSELL
Music by HENRY KRIEGER

Ballad

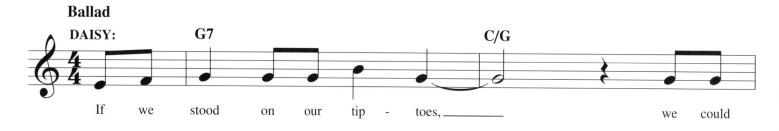

DAISY: If we stood on our tip - toes, _____ we could

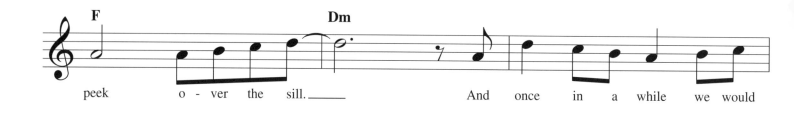

peek o - ver the sill._____ And once in a while we would

see a girl____ slow - ly walk - ing up the hill._____ And we'd

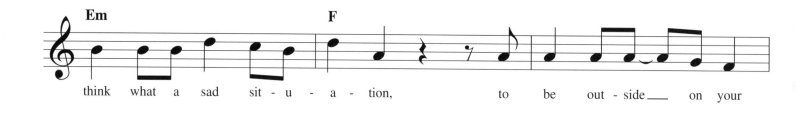

think what a sad sit - u - a - tion, to be out - side____ on your

own, DAISY: to go through the town with no play - mate, VIOLET: to

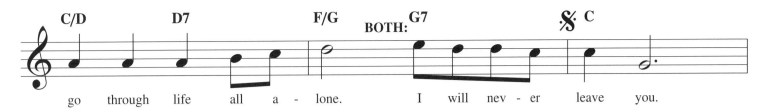

go through life all a - lone. I will nev - er leave you.

I will nev - er go a - way. We were meant to share each

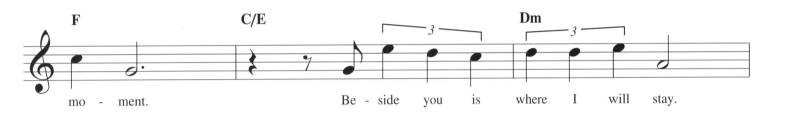

mo - ment. Be - side you is where I will stay.

Ev - er - more and al - ways, we'll be

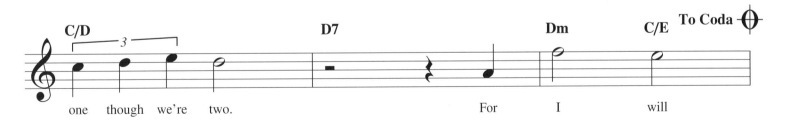

one though we're two. For I will

nev - er leave you. When the

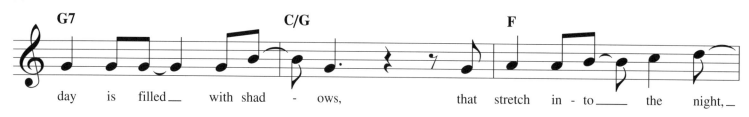

day is filled __ with shad - ows, that stretch in - to __ the night, __

__ I am filled with your sweet com - fort, like

morn - ing fills with light. _____ I will nev - er

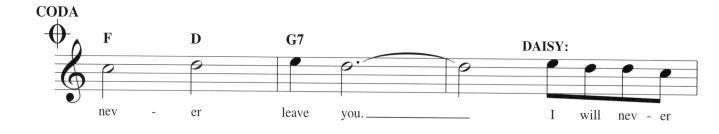

nev - er leave you. _____ I will nev - er

leave you, I will nev - er leave you. I will nev - er

go a - way. __ We were meant to share each mo - ment.

DAISY: Be - side you is where I will stay. That's where VIOLET: I will stay.

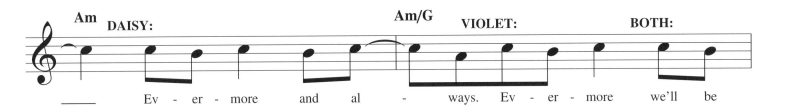

DAISY: ___ Ev - er - more and al - ways. VIOLET: Ev - er - more BOTH: we'll be

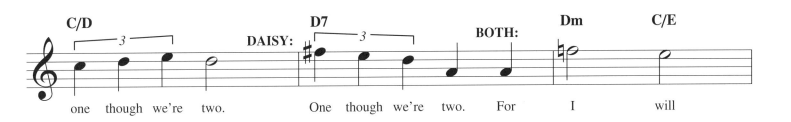

one though we're two. DAISY: One though we're two. BOTH: For I will

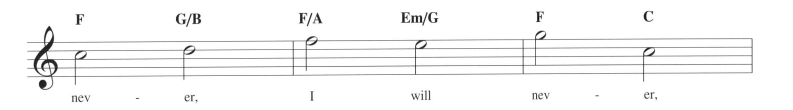

nev - er, I will nev - er,

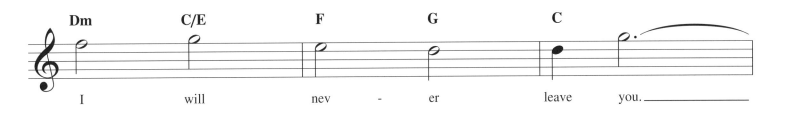

I will nev - er leave you. ___

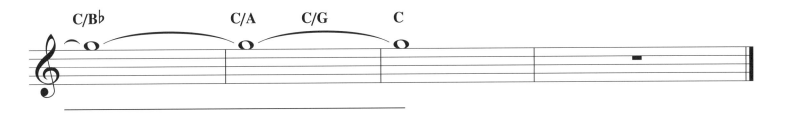

I'LL NEVER FALL IN LOVE AGAIN
from PROMISES, PROMISES

Lyric by HAL DAVID
Music by BURT BACHARACH

What do you get when you fall in love, ___ a

{ guy }
{ girl } with a pin to burst ___ your bub - ble,

that's what you get for all your trou - ble, I'll

nev - er fall in love a - gain. ___

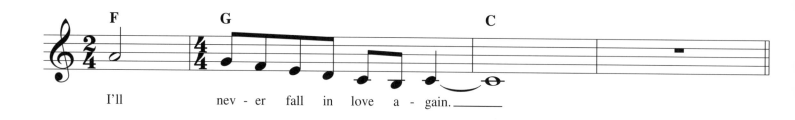

I'll nev - er fall in love a - gain. ___

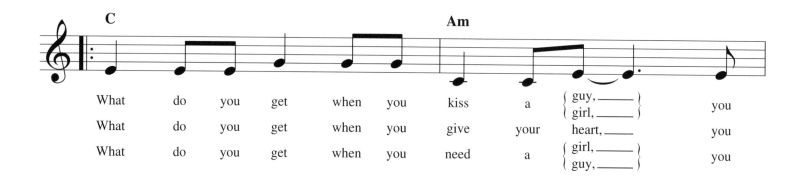

What do you get when you kiss a { guy, ___ } you
{ girl, ___ }
What do you get when you give your heart, ___ you
What do you get when you need a { girl, ___ } you
{ guy, ___ }

F

get e - nough germs to catch_____ pneu - mo - nia,
get it all bro - ken up_____ and bat - tered,
get e - nough tears to fill_____ an o - cean,

Em   **Em/A**   **A7**

af - ter you do, { he'll / she'll } nev - er phone_____ you;
that's what you get, a heart that's shat - tered;
that's what you get for your de - vo - tion;

Dm   **G7**   **F7**

I'll nev - er fall in love a - gain._____

C   **F**   **G**

____ I'll nev - er fall in love a - gain.____

C   **Dm/G**

____ Don't tell me what it's all a - bout,__

C   **Dm/G**

____ 'cause I've been there_____ and I'm

C   **Em**

glad I'm out;_____ out of those chains, those

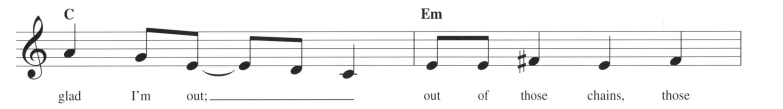

IF I WERE A BELL
from GUYS AND DOLLS

By FRANK LOESSER

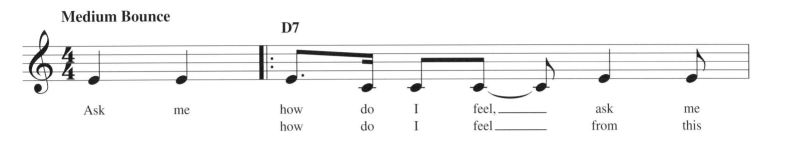

Ask me how do I feel, ask me
how do I feel from this

now that we're co-zy and cling-ing.
chem-is-try les-son I'm learn-ing.

Well sir, all I can say is if I
Well sir, all I can say is if I

were a bell I'd be ring-ing.
were a bridge I'd be burn-ing.

From the mo-ment we kissed to-nite that's the
Yes, I knew my mor-ale would crack from the

way I've just got to be - have. _____ Boy, if
won - der - ful way you looked. _____ Boy, if

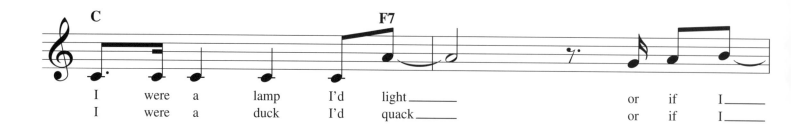

I were a lamp I'd light_____ or if I_____
I were a duck I'd quack_____ or if I_____

_____ were a ban - ner I'd wave._____ Ask me
_____ were a goose_____ I'd be cooked._____ Ask me

how do I feel,_____ lit - tle me with my qui - et up -
how do I feel,_____ ask me now that we're fond - ly ca -

bring - ing. _____ Well sir,
ress - ing. _____ Pal, if

all   I   can   say_____   is   if   I_____   were   a   gate_____   I'd   be

I   were   a   sal -   ad   I   know_____   I'd   be   splash -   ing   my

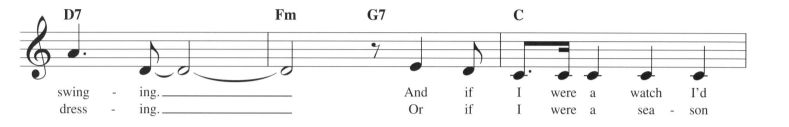

swing -   ing._____   And   if   I   were   a   watch   I'd

dress -   ing._____   Or   if   I   were   a   sea -   son

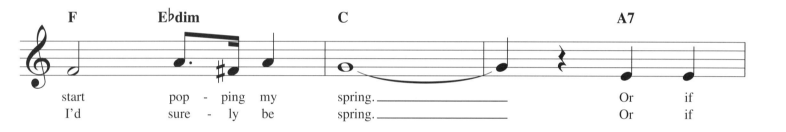

start   pop -   ping   my   spring._____   Or   if

I'd   sure -   ly   be   spring._____   Or   if

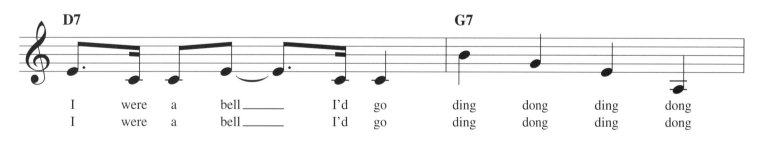

I   were   a   bell_____   I'd   go   ding   dong   ding   dong

I   were   a   bell_____   I'd   go   ding   dong   ding   dong

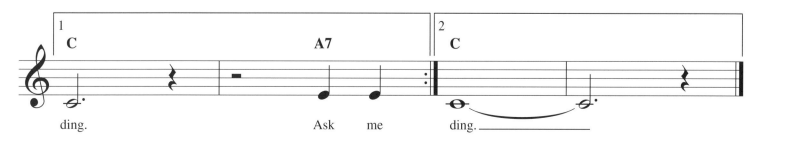

ding.   Ask   me   ding._____

I'M GONNA WASH THAT MAN RIGHT OUTA MY HAIR
from SOUTH PACIFIC

Lyrics by OSCAR HAMMERSTEIN II
Music by RICHARD RODGERS

I'VE GOT YOUR NUMBER
from LITTLE ME

Music by CY COLEMAN
Lyrics by CAROLYN LEIGH

Moderate, with a relaxed swinging beat

I've got your num - ber. _____ I know you
I've got your num - ber. _____ And what you're

in - side _____ out. You ain't no Ea - gle _____ Scout.
look - ing _____ for and what you're look - ing _____ for

You're all at sea! Oh, yes, you'll brag a lot, _____
just suits me fine! We'll break the rules a lot. _____

wave your own _____ flag a lot. _____ But you're un -

sure a lot. _____ You're a lot _____ like me. Oh,

We'll be damn' — fools a lot. ___ But then why

should we not. ___ How could we not ___ com - bine, when

I've got your num - ber ___ and I've got the

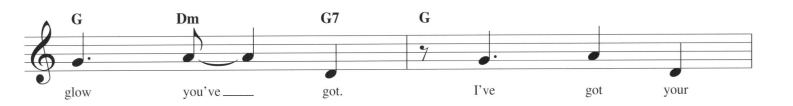

glow you've ___ got. I've got your

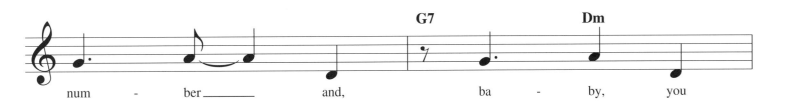

num - ber ___ and, ba - by, you

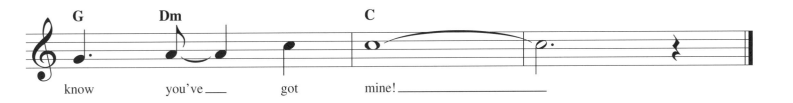

know you've ___ got mine! _____

IF I WERE A RICH MAN
from the Musical FIDDLER ON THE ROOF

Words by SHELDON HARNICK
Music by JERRY BOCK

IT'S A GRAND NIGHT FOR SINGING
from STATE FAIR

Lyrics by OSCAR HAMMERSTEIN II
Music by RICHARD RODGERS

Moderately

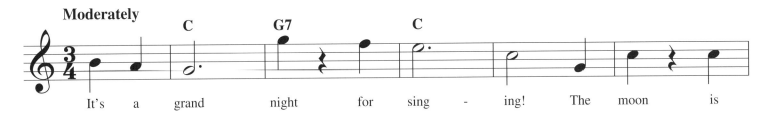

It's a grand night for sing - ing! The moon is

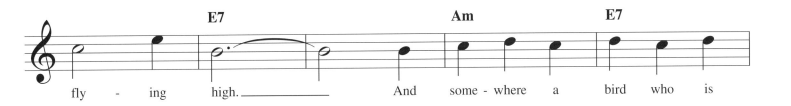

fly - ing high. _____ And some - where a bird who is

bound he'll be heard, is throw - ing his heart at the sky.

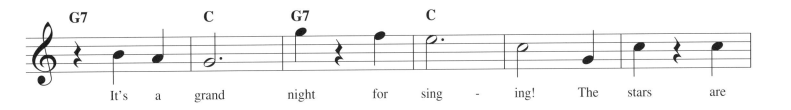

It's a grand night for sing - ing! The stars are

bright a - bove. _____ The earth is a - glow and to add to the

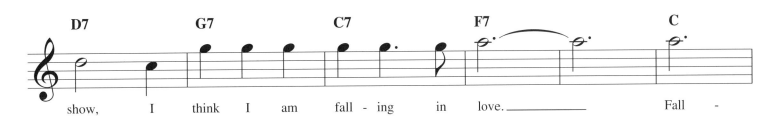

show, I think I am fall - ing in love. _____ Fall -

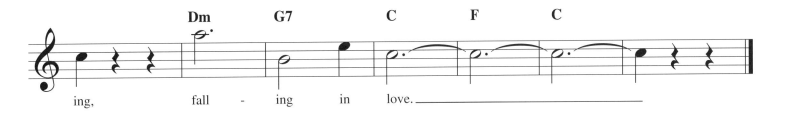

ing, fall - ing in love. _____

IF MY FRIENDS COULD SEE ME NOW
from SWEET CHARITY

Music by CY COLEMAN
Lyrics by DOROTHY FIELDS

Moderately

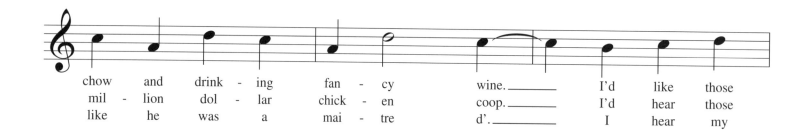

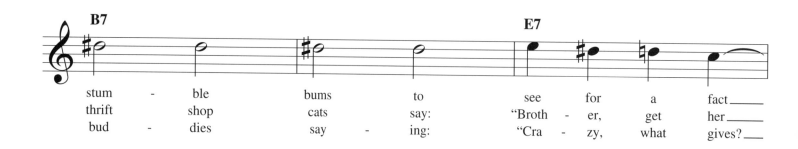

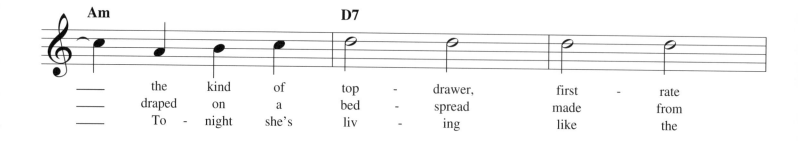

chums   I   at - tract. _____   All   I   can   say   is   "Wow -
three   kinds   of   fur." _____   All   I   can   say   is,   "Wow! ___
oth - er   half   lives." _____   To   think   the   high - est   brow, ___

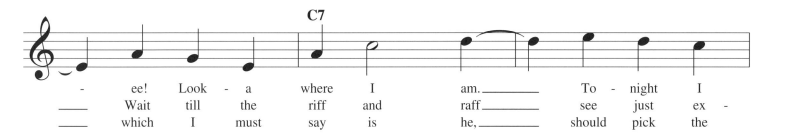

\- ee!   Look - a   where   I   am. _____   To - night   I
____   Wait   till   the   riff   and   raff _____   see   just   ex -
____   which   I   must   say   is   he, _____   should   pick   the

land - ed,   pow, _____   right   in   a   pot   of   jam." ___
act - ly   how _____   he   signed   this   au - to - graph." __
low - est   brow, _____   which   there's   no   doubt   is   me. ___

____   What   a   set   up!   Ho - ly   cow! ___
____   What   a   build - up!   Ho - ly   cow! ___
____   What   a   step   up!   Ho - ly   cow! ___

___   They'd   nev - er   be - lieve   it,   if   my   friends   could

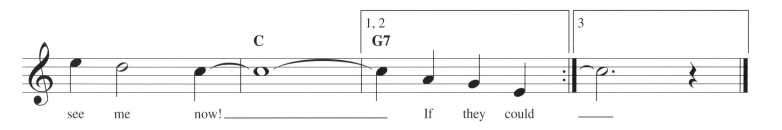

see   me   now! _____   If   they   could   ___

IT DON'T MEAN A THING
(If It Ain't Got That Swing)
from SOPHISTICATED LADIES
featured in the Broadway Musical SWING!

Words and Music by DUKE ELLINGTON
and IRVING MILLS

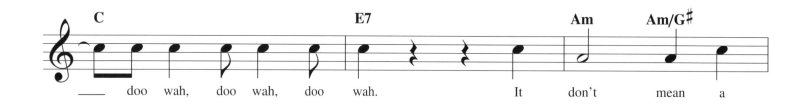

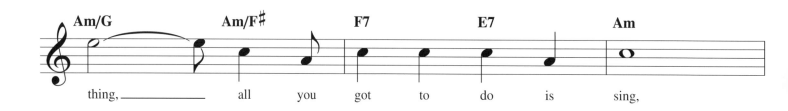

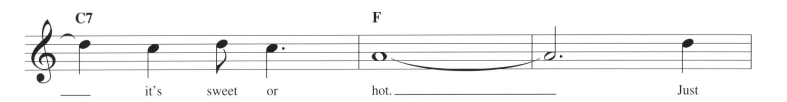

it's   sweet   or   hot.   Just

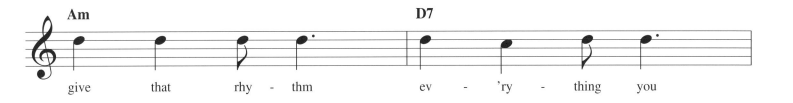

give   that   rhy - thm   ev - 'ry - thing   you

got.   It   don't   mean   a

thing   if   it   ain't   got   that   swing,____

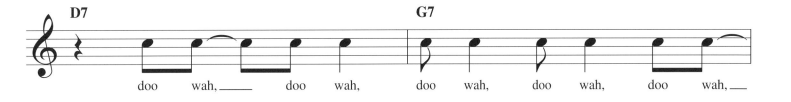

doo   wah,____   doo   wah,   doo   wah,   doo   wah,   doo   wah,____

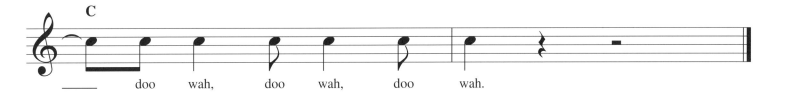

____   doo   wah,   doo   wah,   doo   wah.

IT ONLY TAKES A MOMENT

from HELLO, DOLLY!

Music and Lyric by
JERRY HERMAN

Moderately

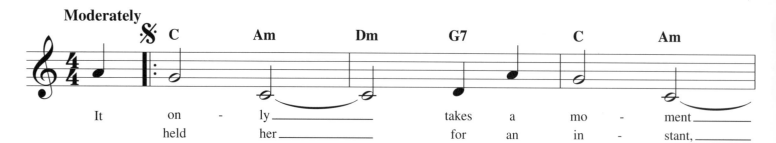

It on - ly _____ takes a mo - ment _____
held her _____ for an in - stant, _____

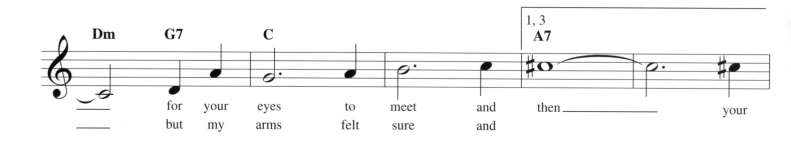

for your eyes to meet and then _____ your
but my arms to felt sure and

heart knows _____ in a mo - ment _____ you will

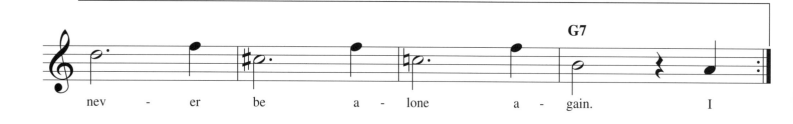

nev - er be a - lone a - gain. I

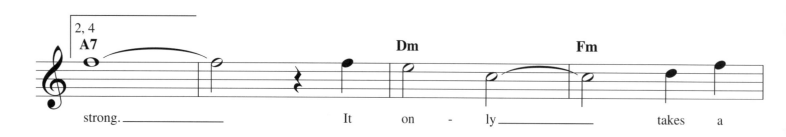

strong. _____ It on - ly _____ takes a

mo - ment _____ to be loved a whole life

IT'S A LOVELY DAY TODAY
from the Stage Production CALL ME MADAM

Words and Music by
IRVING BERLIN

Moderately

It's a love - ly day to - day._____ So what -

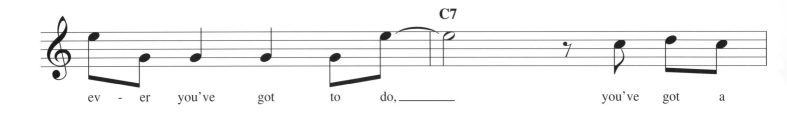

ev - er you've got to do,_____ you've got a

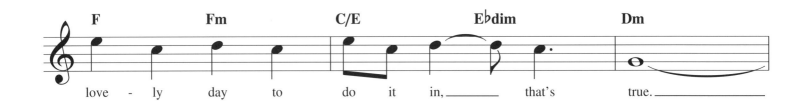

love - ly day to do it in,_____ that's true._____

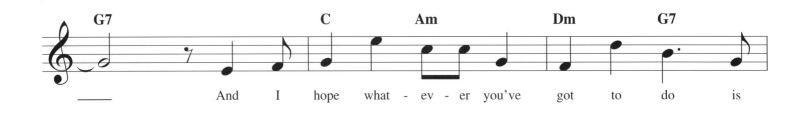

_____ And I hope what - ev - er you've got to do is

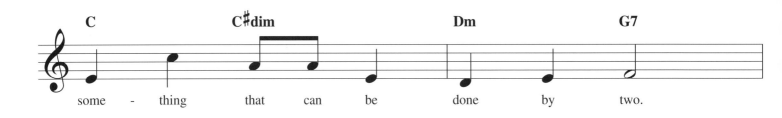

some - thing that can be done by two.

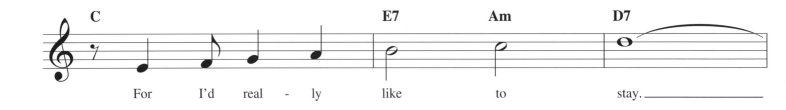

For I'd real - ly like to stay._____

It's a love-ly day to-day.____ And what-

ev-er you've got to do,____ I'd be so hap-py to be

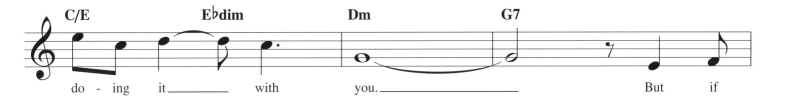

do-ing it____ with you._____ But if

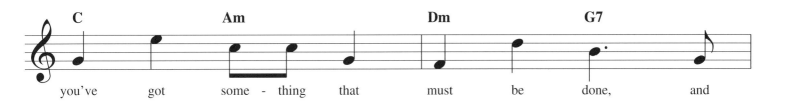

you've got some-thing that must be done, and

it can on-ly be done by one, there is noth-ing

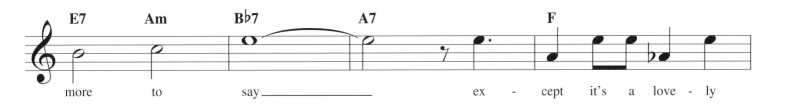

more to say_____ ex - cept it's a love-ly

day for say-ing it's a love-ly day.

IT'S ALL RIGHT WITH ME
from CAN-CAN
from HIGH SOCIETY

Words and Music by
COLE PORTER

Moderately fast

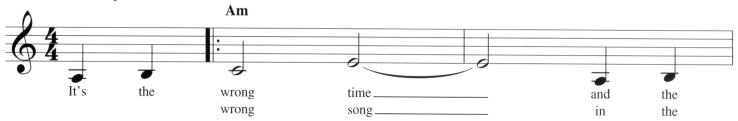

It's the wrong time_____ and the
wrong song_____ in the

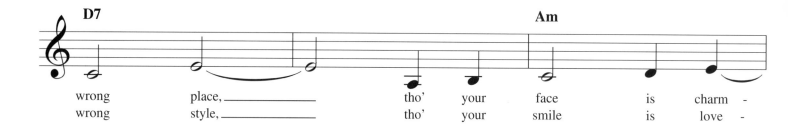

wrong place,_____ tho' your face is charm -
wrong style,_____ tho' your smile is love -

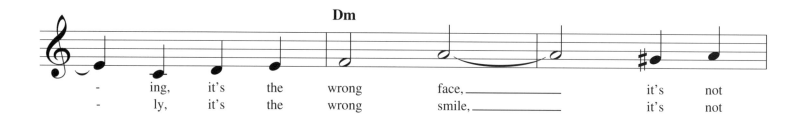

- ing, it's the wrong face,_____ it's not
- ly, it's the wrong smile,_____ it's not

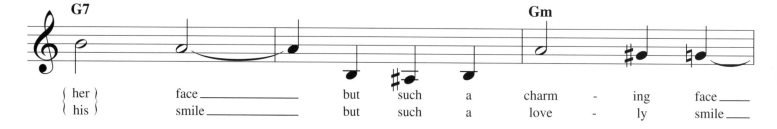

{ her } face_____ but such a charm - ing face_____
{ his } smile_____ but such a love - ly smile_____

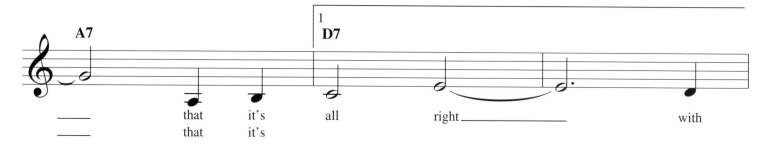

that it's all right_____ with
that it's

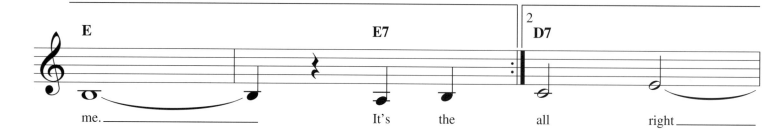

me. It's the all right_____

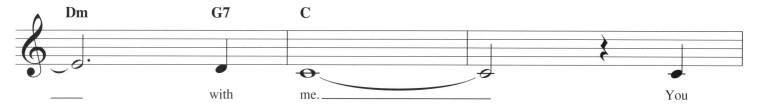

_____ with me. _____ You

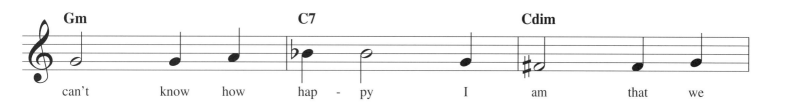

can't know how hap - py I am that we

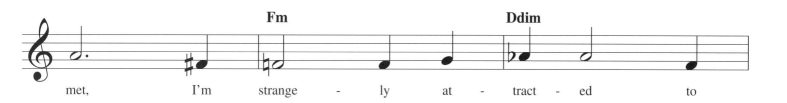

met, I'm strange - ly at - tract - ed to

you. _____ There's some - one I'm

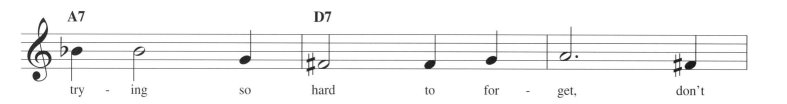

try - ing so hard to for - get, don't

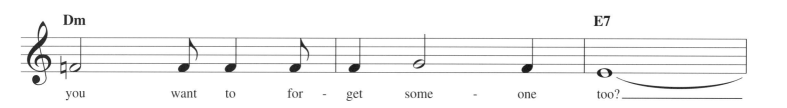

you want to for - get some - one too? _____

_____ It's the wrong game _____ with the

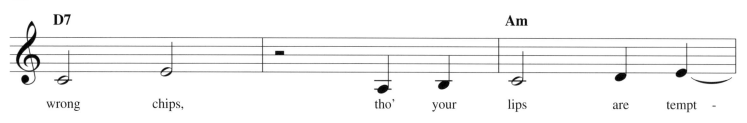

wrong   chips,   tho' your   lips   are   tempt -

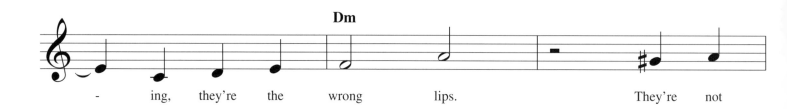

- ing,   they're   the   wrong   They're   not
                                            lips.

{ her }
{ his }   lips,   but   they're   such   tempt - ing   lips___

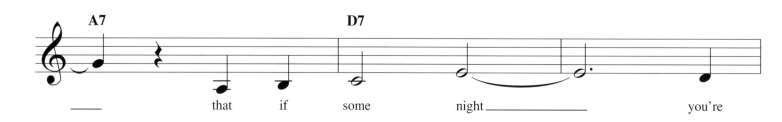

___   that   if   some   night_____   you're

free,_____   dear,   it's   all   right,_____

___   it's   all   right_____   with

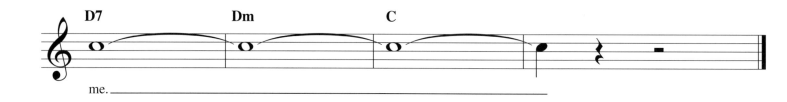

me._____

A LITTLE FALL OF RAIN
from LES MISÉRABLES

Music by CLAUDE-MICHEL SCHÖNBERG
Lyrics by ALAIN BOUBLIL,
JEAN-MARC NATEL and HERBERT KRETZMER

love. Just hold me now and let it be. Shel - ter me,

com - fort me. You would live_____ a hun - dred years___ if

I could show you how. I won't de - sert you now. The

rain can't___ hurt me now. This rain will wash a - way what's

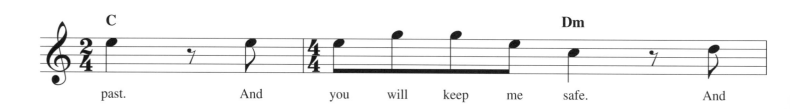

past. And you will keep me safe. And

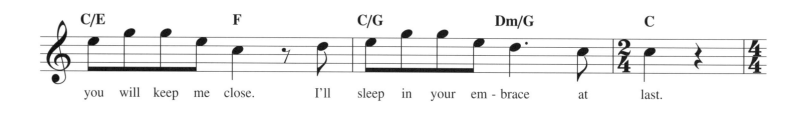

you will keep me close. I'll sleep in your em - brace at last.

The rain that brings you here is heav - en blessed. The skies be -

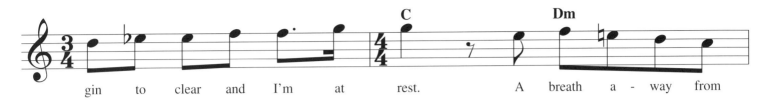

gin to clear and I'm at rest. A breath a - way from

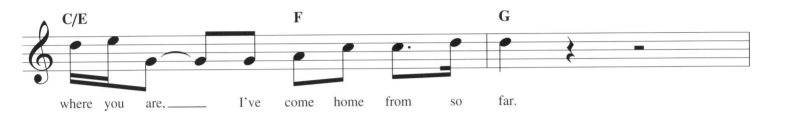

where you are,_____ I've come home from so far.

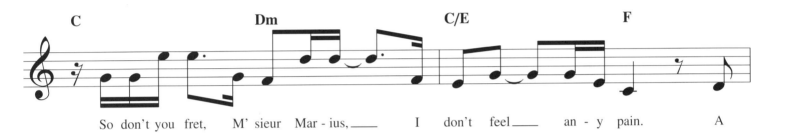

So don't you fret, M' sieur Mar - ius,_____ I don't feel____ an - y pain. A

lit - tle fall of rain can hard - ly hurt me now. I'm

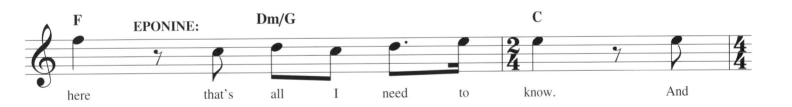

here that's all I need to know. And

you will keep me safe. And you will keep me close. And

rain will make the flow - ers... grow.

IT'S DE-LOVELY
from RED, HOT AND BLUE!

Words and Music by
COLE PORTER

The night is young, ___ the skies are clear ___ and

if you want ___ to go walk - ing, dear, ___ it's de -

light - ful, ___ it's de - li - cious, ___ it's de - love - ly. ___

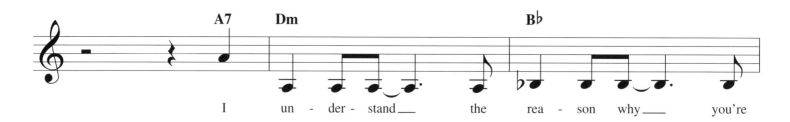

I un - der - stand ___ the rea - son why ___ you're

sen - ti - men - tal, 'cause so am I, ___ it's de - light - ful, ___ it's de -

li - cious, ___ it's de - love - ly. ___ You can

tell at a glance ___ what a swell night ___ this

is for ro - mance.___ You can hear dear Moth - er

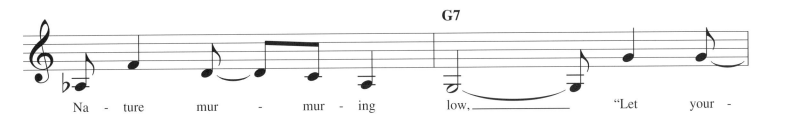

Na - ture mur - mur - ing low,_____ "Let your -

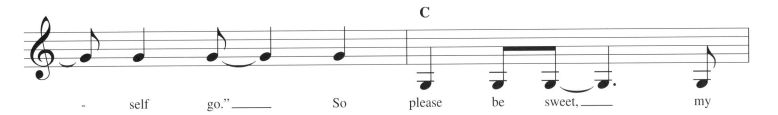

- self go."_____ So please be sweet,_____ my

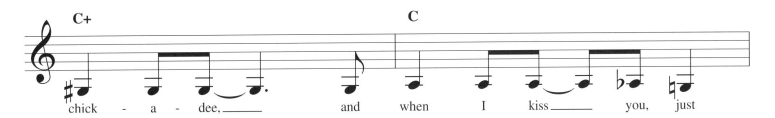

chick - a - dee,_____ and when I kiss_____ you, just

say to me,_____ "It's de - light - ful,_____ it's de -

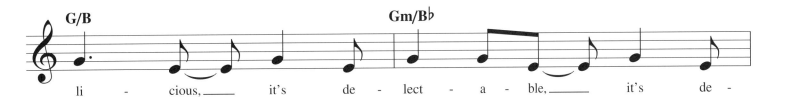

li - cious,_____ it's de - lect - a - ble,_____ it's de -

lir - i - ous,_____ it's di - lem - ma, it's_____ de - li - mit,

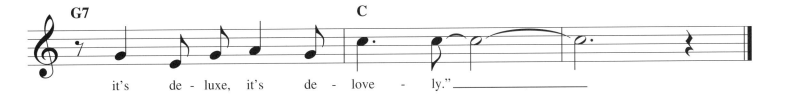

it's de - luxe, it's de - love - ly."_____

JOEY, JOEY, JOEY
from THE MOST HAPPY FELLA

By FRANK LOESSER

Jo - ey,_____ Jo - ey Jo - ey,_____
Jo - ey,_____ Jo - ey Jo - ey,_____

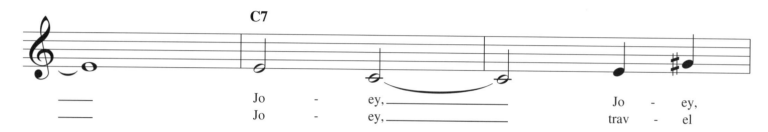

_____ Jo - ey,_____ Jo - ey,
_____ Jo - ey,_____ trav - el

Joe._____ You've been too long_____
on._____ You've been too long_____

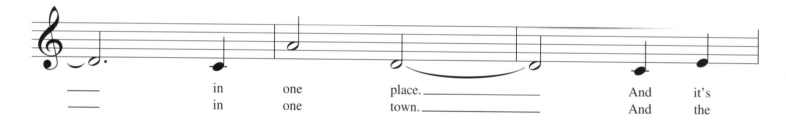

_____ in one place._____ And it's
_____ in one town._____ And the

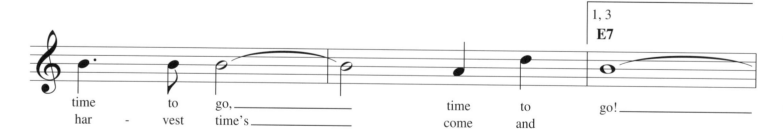

time to go,_____ time to go!_____
har - vest time's_____ come to and

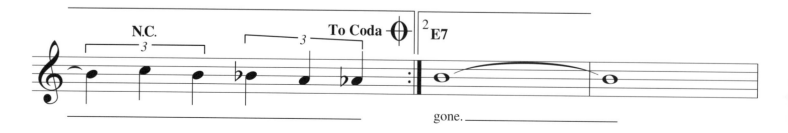

gone._____

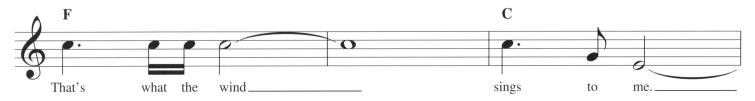

Thats what the wind _____ sings to me. _____

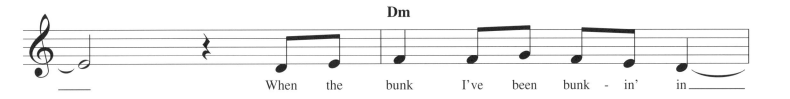

____ When the bunk I've been bunk - in' in _____

____ gets to feel - in' too soft and co - zy, _____ when the

grub they've been cook - in' me _____ gets to tast - in' too

good. _____ When I've had all I want of the

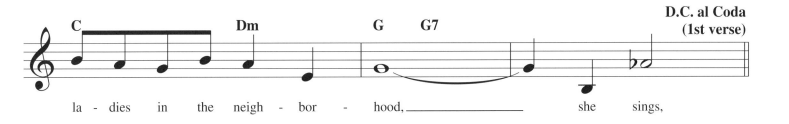

la - dies in the neigh - bor - hood, _____ she sings,

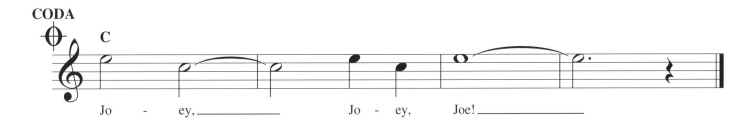

Jo - ey, _____ Jo - ey, Joe! _____

LIDA ROSE
from Meredith Willson's THE MUSIC MAN

By MEREDITH WILLSON

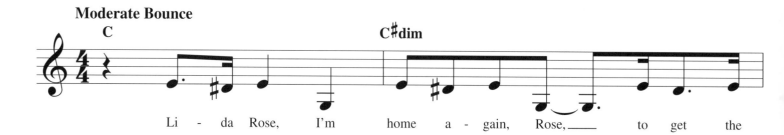

Li - da Rose, I'm home a - gain, Rose, _____ to get the

sun back in my sky. Li - da Rose, I'm

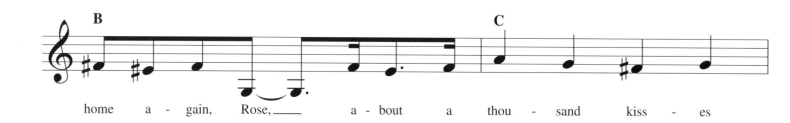

home a - gain, Rose, _____ a - bout a thou - sand kiss - es

shy. Ding, dong, ding! I can

hear the chap - el bell chime. Ding, dong,

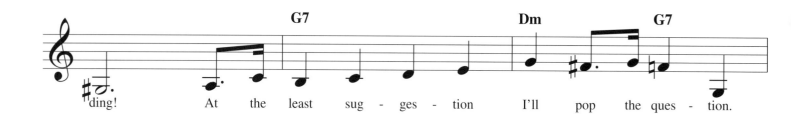

ding! At the least sug - ges - tion I'll pop the ques - tion.

Li - da Rose, I'm home a - gain, Rose, with - out a

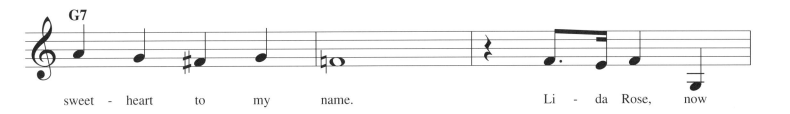

sweet - heart to my name. Li - da Rose, now

ev - 'ry - one knows that I am hop - ing you're the same.

So here is my love song,

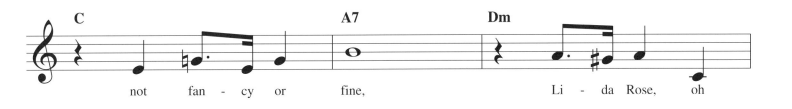

not fan - cy or fine, Li - da Rose, oh

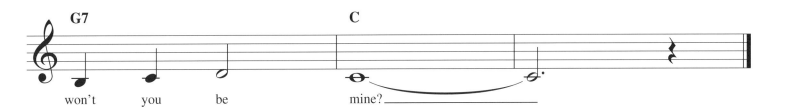

won't you be mine?

LITTLE GIRL BLUE
from JUMBO

Words by LORENZ HART
Music by RICHARD RODGERS

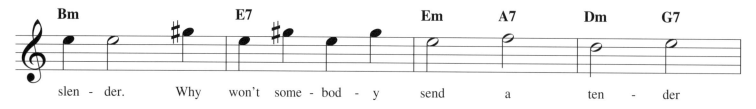

LOST IN THE STARS

from the Musical Production LOST IN THE STARS

Words by MAXWELL ANDERSON
Music by KURT WEILL

Moderately

Be - fore Lord God made the sea and the land, He

held all the stars in the palm of His hand. And they

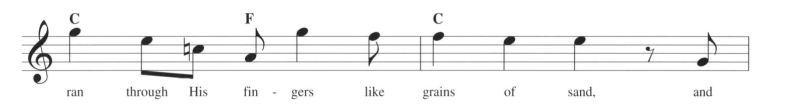

ran through His fin - gers like grains of sand, and

one lit - tle star fell a - lone. Then the

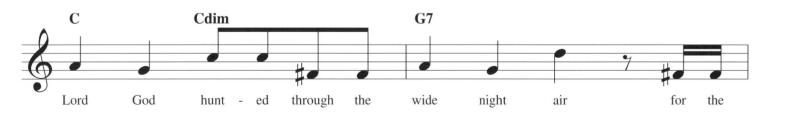

Lord God hunt - ed through the wide night air for the

lit - tle dark star on the wind down___ there. And He

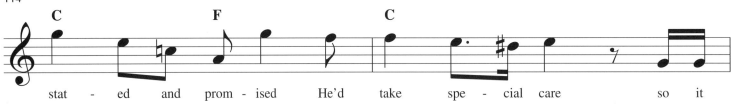

stat - ed and prom - ised He'd take spe - cial care so it

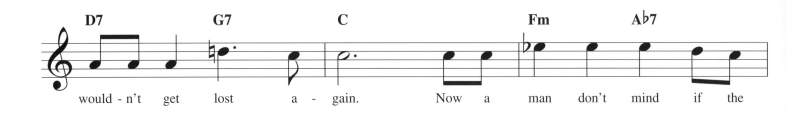

would - n't get lost a - gain. Now a man don't mind if the

stars grow dim and the clouds blow o - ver and

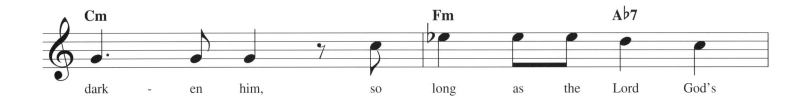

dark - en him, so long as the Lord God's

watch - ing o - ver them, keep - ing track how it all goes

on. But I've been walk - ing through the

night and the day till my eyes get wea - ry and my

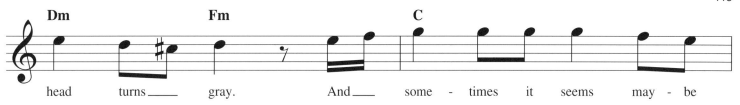

head turns ___ gray. And ___ some - times it seems may - be

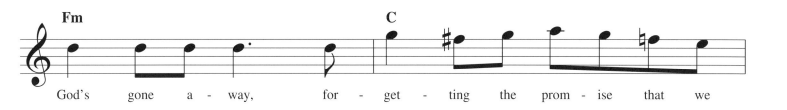

God's gone a - way, for - get - ting the prom - ise that we

heard Him say. And we're lost out here in the stars,

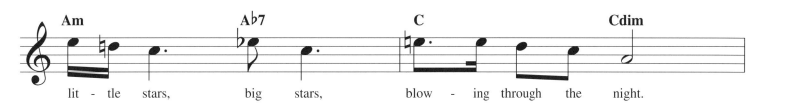

lit - tle stars, big stars, blow - ing through the night.

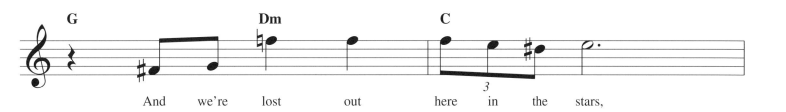

And we're lost out here in the stars,

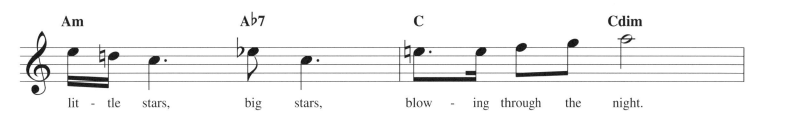

lit - tle stars, big stars, blow - ing through the night.

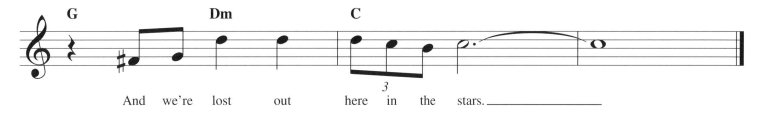

And we're lost out here in the stars. _____

LOOK FOR THE SILVER LINING
from SALLY

Words by BUDDY DeSYLVA
Music by JEROME KERN

Smoothly

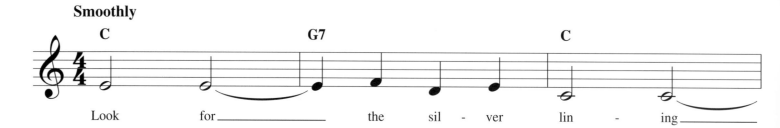

Look for the sil - ver lin - ing

when - e'er a cloud ap - pears in the

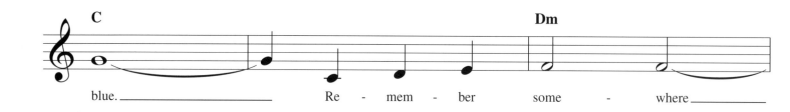

blue. Re - mem - ber some - where

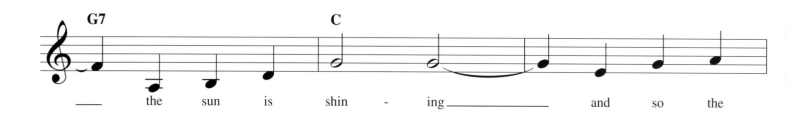

the sun is shin - ing and so the

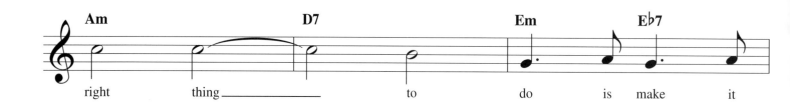

right thing to do is make it

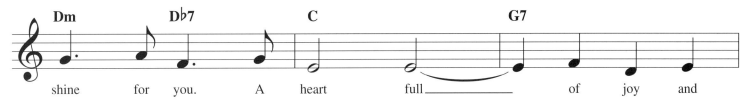

shine for you. A heart full_____ of joy and

glad - ness_____ will al - ways ban - ish

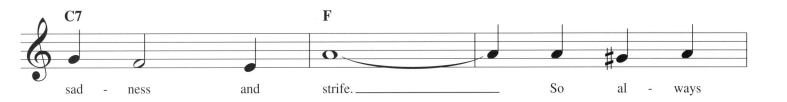

sad - ness and strife._____ So al - ways

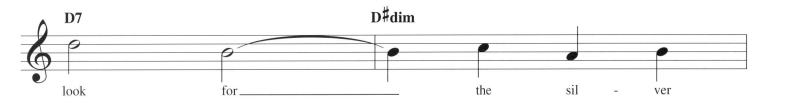

look for_____ the sil - ver

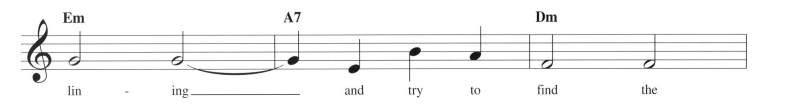

lin - ing_____ and try to find the

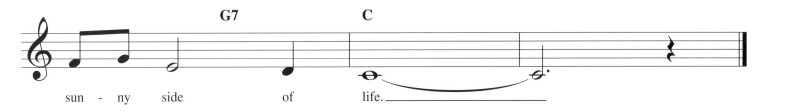

sun - ny side of life._____

LOVE CHANGES EVERYTHING
from ASPECTS OF LOVE

Music by ANDREW LLOYD WEBBER
Lyrics by DON BLACK and CHARLES HART

Drammatico

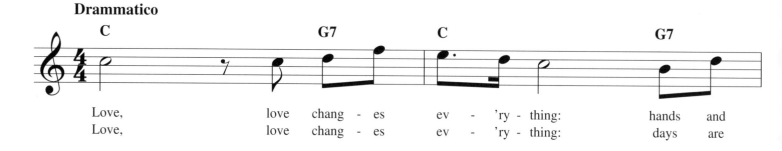

Love,   love chang - es   ev - 'ry - thing: hands and
Love,   love chang - es   ev - 'ry - thing: days   are

fac - es,   earth and   sky.   Love,   love chang - es
long - er,   words mean more.   Love,   love chang - es

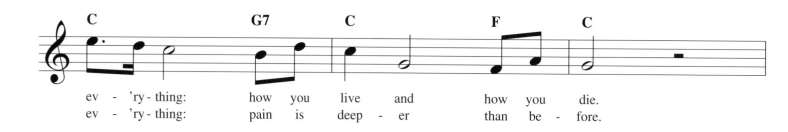

ev - 'ry - thing: how   you   live   and   how   you   die.
ev - 'ry - thing: pain is   deep - er   than be - fore.

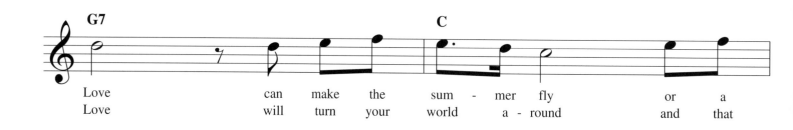

Love   can make   the   sum - mer fly   or   a
Love   will turn   your world a - round   and that

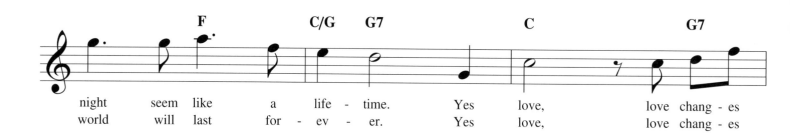

night seem like   a   life - time.   Yes love,   love chang - es
world will last   for - ev - er.   Yes love,   love chang - es

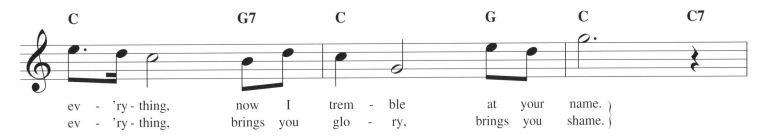

ev - 'ry - thing,   now I trem - ble   at your name.
ev - 'ry - thing,   brings you glo - ry,   brings you shame.

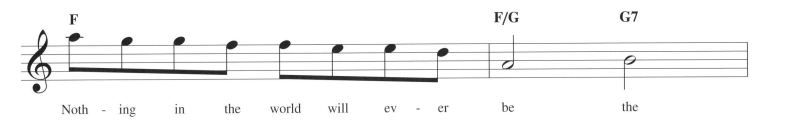

Noth - ing in the world will ev - er be   the

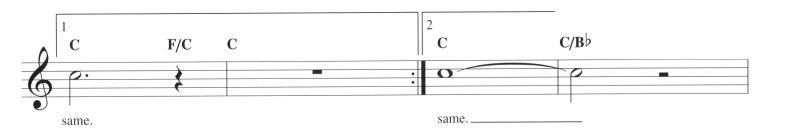

same.   same.

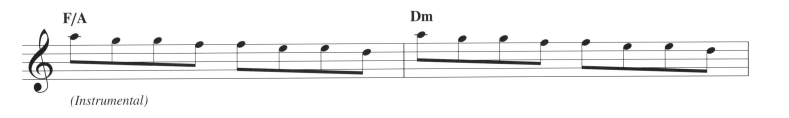

(Instrumental)

Off   in - to the

world we go,   plan - ning fu - tures,   shap - ing years.

Love_____ bursts in and sud - den - ly all our wis - dom dis - ap -

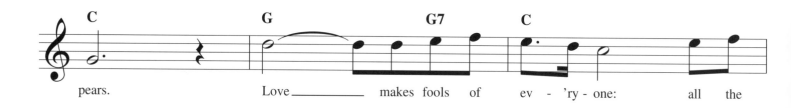

pears. Love_____ makes fools of ev - 'ry - one: all the

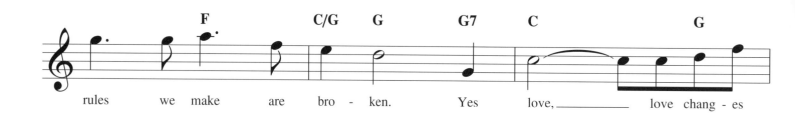

rules we make are bro - ken. Yes love,_____ love chang - es

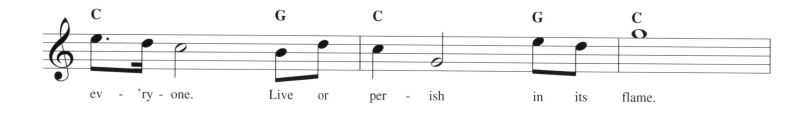

ev - 'ry - one. Live or per - ish in its flame.

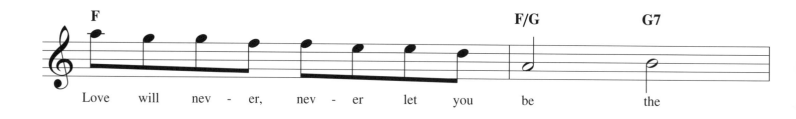

Love will nev - er, nev - er let you be the

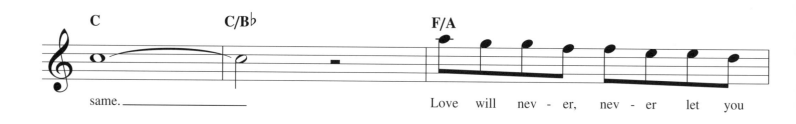

same._____ Love will nev - er, nev - er let you

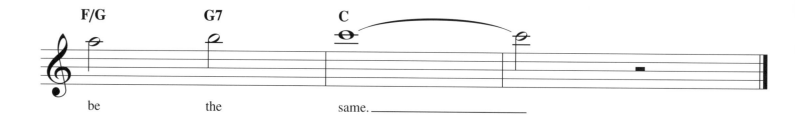

be the same._____

MAKE BELIEVE
from SHOW BOAT

Lyrics by OSCAR HAMMERSTEIN II
Music by JEROME KERN

Moderately slow

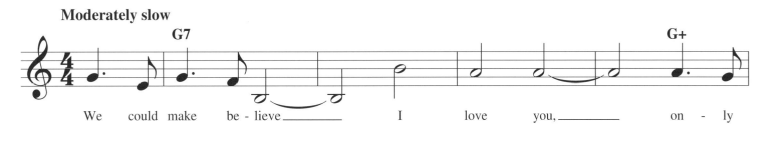

We could make be-lieve_____ I love you,_____ on-ly

make be-lieve_____ that you love me._____ Oth-ers

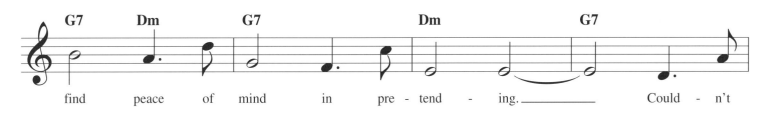

find peace of mind in pre-tend-ing._____ Could-n't

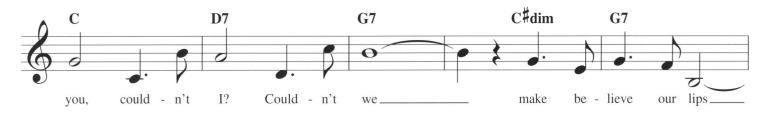

you, could-n't I? Could-n't we_____ make be-lieve our lips_____

_____ are blend-ing_____ in a phan-tom kiss,_____ or two, or

three?_____ Might as well make be-lieve I love you,_____

_____ for to tell the truth,_____ I do._____

LOVE, LOOK AWAY
from FLOWER DRUM SONG

Lyrics by OSCAR HAMMERSTEIN II
Music by RICHARD RODGERS

Moderately, with expression

Love look a - way!_____ Love look a - way from

me. Fly when you pass my door,

fly and get lost at sea. Call it a day._____

_____ Love, let us say we're through.

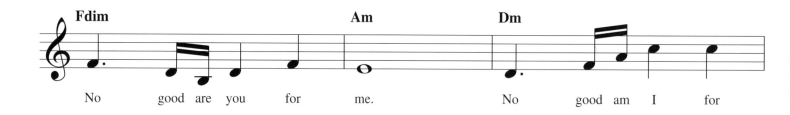

No good are you for me. No good am I for

you. Want - ing you_____ so, I

123

try too much._____ Af - ter you_____

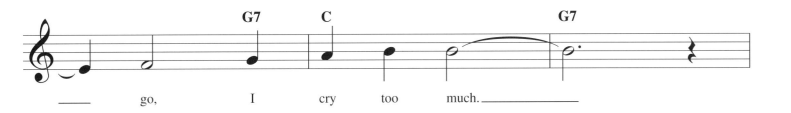

_____ go, I cry too much._____

Love, look a - way._____ Lone - ly though I may

be, leave me and set me

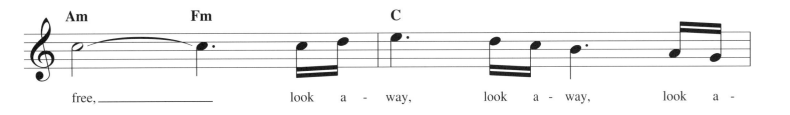

free,_____ look a - way, look a - way, look a -

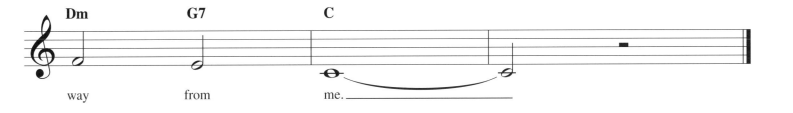

way from me._____

MAMA, I'M A BIG GIRL NOW
from HAIRSPRAY

Music by MARC SHAIMAN
Lyrics by MARC SHAIMAN and SCOTT WITTMAN

Freely

MOTHERS: PENNY: Stop! Stop tell-ing me what to do-oo. MOTHERS: AMBER: Don't! Don't treat me like a

MOTHERS: TRACY: child of two-oo. No! I know that you want what's best.___

MOTHERS: TRACY: Please! But moth-er please, give it a rest!!!___ TRACY, AMBER & PENNY: A fun shuffle (Instrumental)

MOTHERS: ALL (D.S.): Stop! Don't! No! GIRLS: Please!___

MOTHERS: ___ Stop! Don't No! GIRLS: Please!___

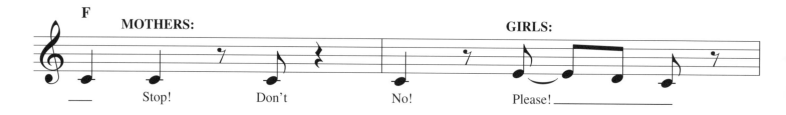

MOTHERS: ___ Stop! Don't No! GIRLS: Please!___

Ma-ma, I'm a big girl now! (Hey, ma-ma, say, ma-ma)

C

(1&3)TRACY (2)AMBER:

Once up - on a time when I was just a kid,_____ you
Once up - on a time I used to play with toys,_____ but
Once up - on a time I was a shy young thing._____ Could

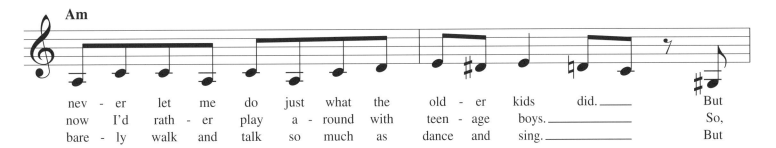

Am

nev - er let me do just what the old - er kids did._____ But
now I'd rath - er play a - round with teen - age boys._____ So,
bare - ly walk and talk so much as dance and sing._____ But

F

lose that laun - dry list of what you won't al - low,_____
if I get a hick - ey, please don't have a cow,_____ } 'cause
let me hit the stage, I wan - na take my bow,_____

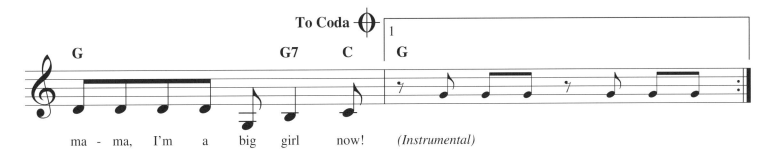

To Coda ⊕   1

G   **G7**   **C**   **G**

ma - ma, I'm a big girl now!   *(Instrumental)*

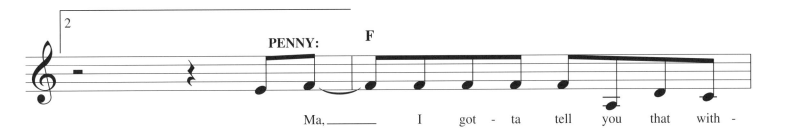

2

PENNY: **F**

Ma,_____ I got - ta tell you that with -

C

out a doubt I get my best danc - ing les - sons from you -

F

-oo. You're ___ the one who taught me how to

D

"Twist and Shout," ___ be - cause you shout non - stop and you're so

Am **G** **Am** **G** *3* *3*

twist - ed ___ too - oo! Wo - oh - oh - oh - oh!

C
TRACY: AMBER:

Once I used to fid - get 'cause I just sat home. ___ But

Am
PENNY:

now I'm just like Gid - get and I got - ta get to Rome! ___ So

F
TRACY: AMBER: GIRLS:

say *ar - ri - ve - der - ci!* Too - dle - oo! And *ciao!* ___ 'Cause

G **G7** **C** **G** D.S. al Coda
ALL:

ma - ma, I'm a big girl now! Oh - oh - oh!

128

MORE I CANNOT WISH YOU
from GUYS AND DOLLS

By FRANK LOESSER

Slowly

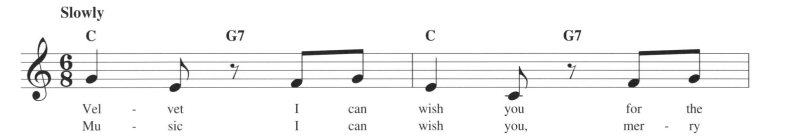

Vel - vet I can wish you for the
Mu - sic I can wish you, mer - ry

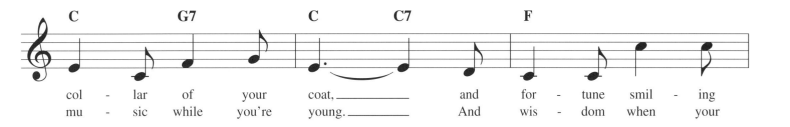

col - lar of your coat,_____ and for - tune smil - ing
mu - sic while you're young._____ And wis - dom when your

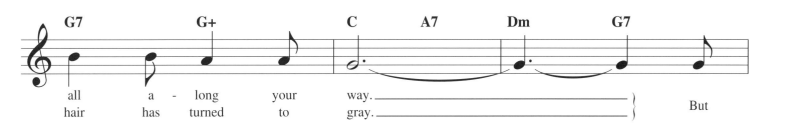

all a - long your way._____
hair has turned to gray._____ But

more I can - not wish you than to wish you find your

To Coda

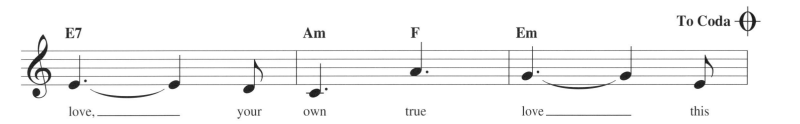

love,_____ your own true love_____ this

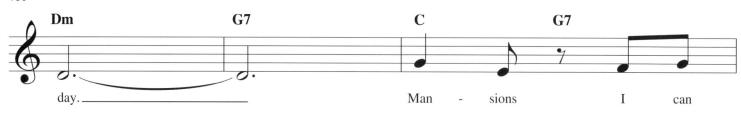

day._____ Man - sions I can

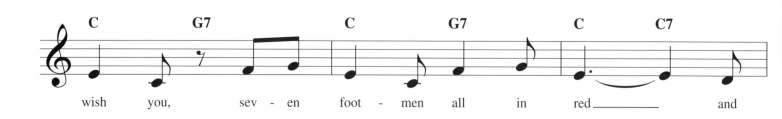

wish you, sev - en foot - men all in red_____ and

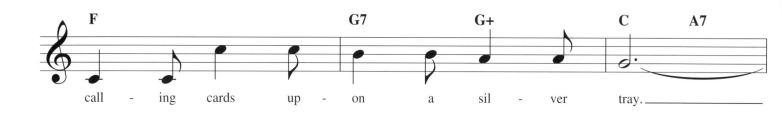

call - ing cards up - on a sil - ver tray._____

_____ But more I can - not wish you than to

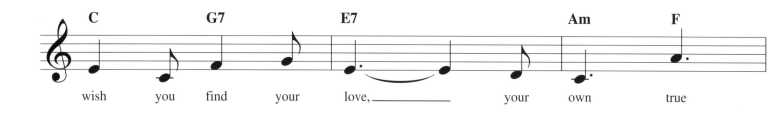

wish you find your love,_____ your own true

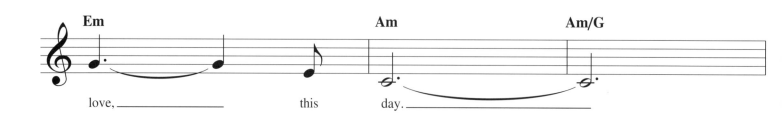

love,_____ this day._____

Stand - ing there_____ gaz - ing at you,_____

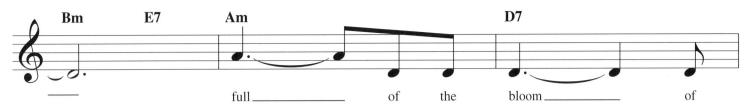

full _____ of the bloom _____ of

youth. _____ Stand - ing there _____

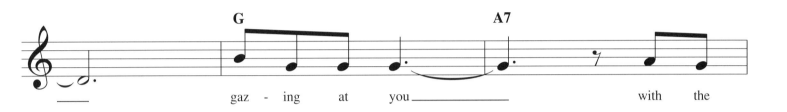

_____ gaz - ing at you _____ with the

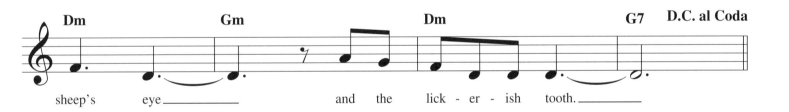

sheep's eye _____ and the lick - er - ish tooth. _____

day. _____ With the sheep's eye and the

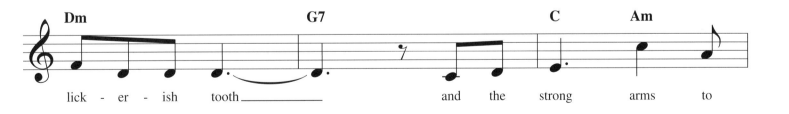

lick - er - ish tooth _____ and the strong arms to

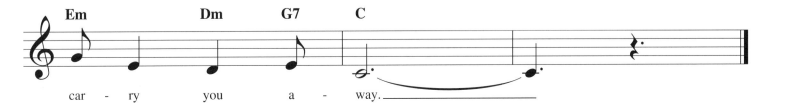

car - ry you a - way. _____

MAMMA MIA
from MAMMA MIA!

Words and Music by BENNY ANDERSSON,
BJÖRN ULVAEUS and STIG ANDERSON

Moderately bright

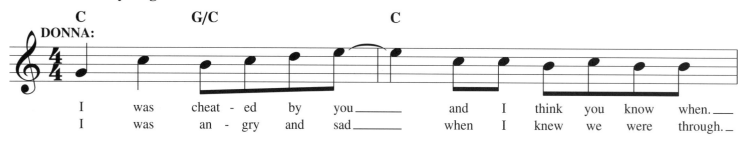

DONNA:

I was cheat-ed by you ___ and I think you know when. ___
I was an - gry and sad ___ when I knew we were through. ___

___ (Instrumental)
___

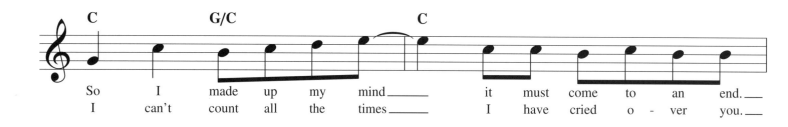

So I made up my mind ___ it must come to an end. ___
I can't count all the times ___ I have cried o - ver you. ___

___ } Instrumental
___

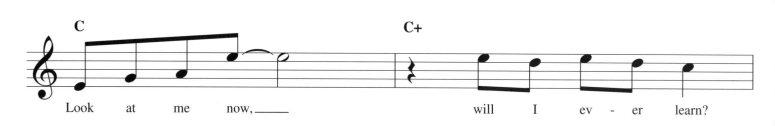

Look at me now, ___ will I ev - er learn?

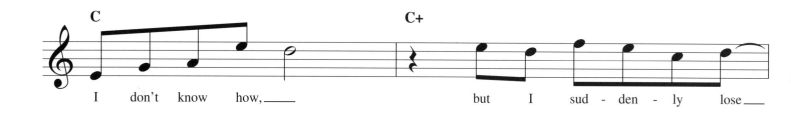

I don't know how, ___ but I sud - den - ly lose ___

con - trol. _____ There's a fire___ with - in_____ my soul. ___

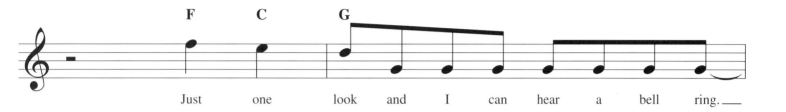

Just one look and I can hear a bell ring. ___

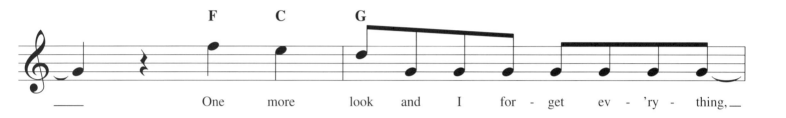

___ One more look and I for - get ev - 'ry - thing, ___

___ oh, _____ oh. _____ Mam - ma Mi - a,

here I go a - gain. ___ My, my how ___

___ can I re - sist ya? Mam - ma Mi - a,

does it show a - gain, ___ my, my, just___

how much I've missed ya? Yes,_____ I've been bro -

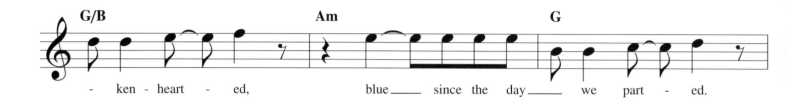

- ken - heart - ed, blue____ since the day____ we part - ed.

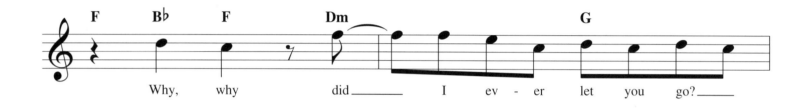

Why, why did_____ I ev - er let you go?____

Mam - ma Mi - a, now I real - ly know,__ my, my, I__

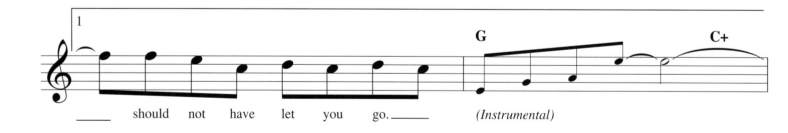

____ should not have let you go._____ *(Instrumental)*

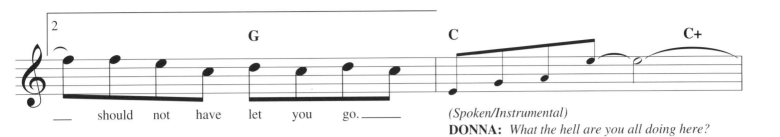

should not have let you go.

(Spoken/Instrumental)
DONNA: *What the hell are you all doing here?*

Well, I'd love to stop and chat, but I have to go and clean out my handbag or something. **BILL:** *Age does not wither her.*

HARRY: *I was expecting a rather stout matron.* **SAM:** *No, she's still Donna.*

Just one look and I can hear a bell ring. One more

look and I for-get ev-'ry-thing, oh, oh.

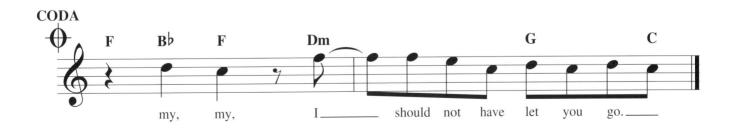

my, my, I should not have let you go.

MASTER OF THE HOUSE
from LES MISÉRABLES

Music by CLAUDE-MICHEL SCHÖNBERG
Lyrics by HERBERT KRETZMER
Original Text by ALAIN BOUBLIL and JEAN-MARC NATEL

137

139

THE MOST BEAUTIFUL GIRL IN THE WORLD
from JUMBO

Words by LORENZ HART
Music by RICHARD RODGERS

The most beau - ti - ful girl in the world ____

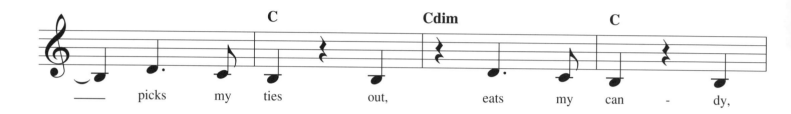

____ picks my ties out, eats my can - dy,

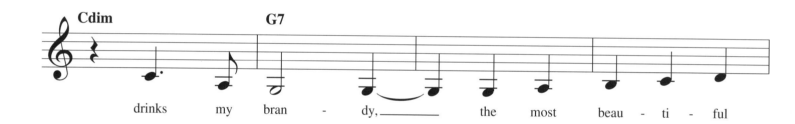

drinks my bran - dy, ____ the most beau - ti - ful

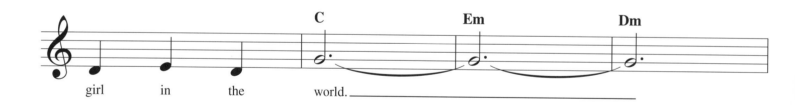

girl in the world. ____

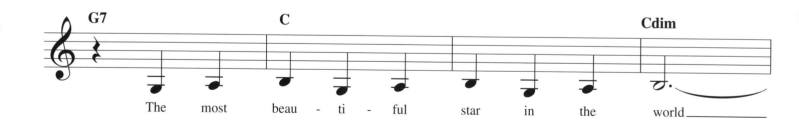

The most beau - ti - ful star in the world ____

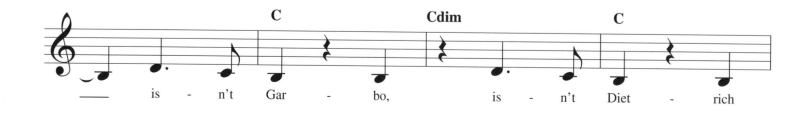

____ is - n't Gar - bo, is - n't Diet - rich

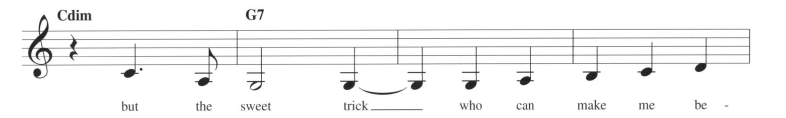

but the sweet trick _____ who can make me be -

lieve it's a beau - ti - ful world. _____

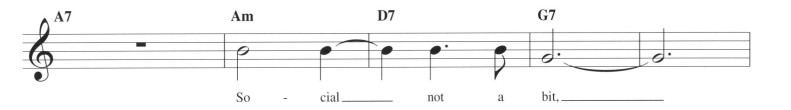

So - cial _____ not a bit, _____

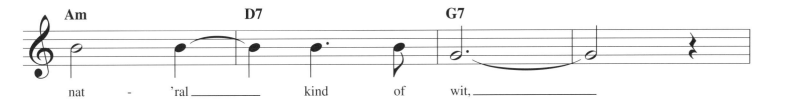

nat - 'ral _____ kind of wit, _____

she'd shine _____ an - y - where, _____ and she

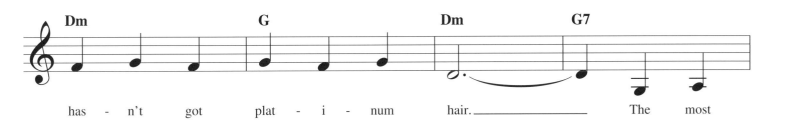

has - n't got plat - i - num hair. _____ The most

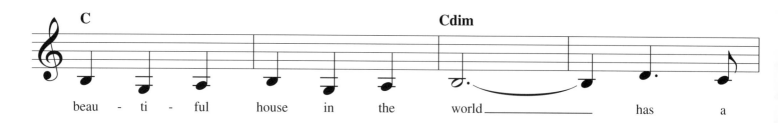

beau - ti - ful house in the world_____ has a

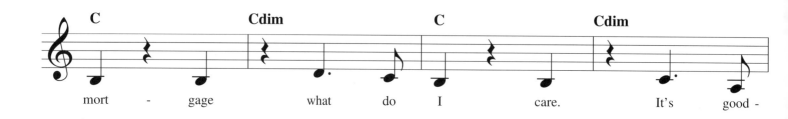

mort - gage what do I care. It's good-

bye care_____ when my slip - pers are next to the

ones that be - long_____ to the

one and on - ly beau - ti - ful

girl in the world!_____

ON MY OWN
from LES MISÉRABLES

Music by CLAUDE-MICHEL SCHÖNBERG
Lyrics by ALAIN BOUBLIL, JOHN CAIRD,
TREVOR NUNN, JEAN-MARC NATEL
and HERBERT KRETZMER

Slowly

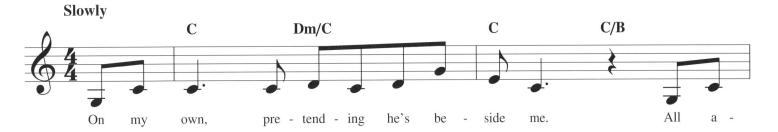

On my own, pre-tend-ing he's be-side me. All a-

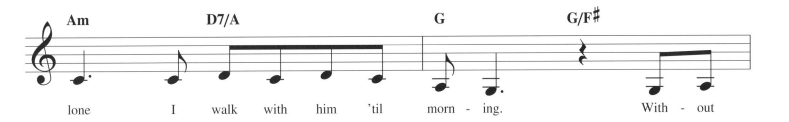

lone I walk with him 'til morn-ing. With-out

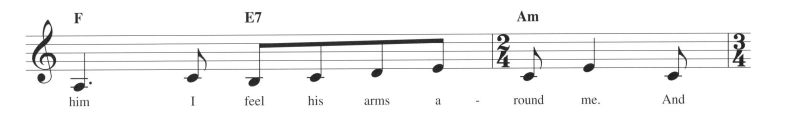

him I feel his arms a-round me. And

when I lose my way I close my eyes and he has found me. In the

rain, the pave-ment shines like sil-ver. All the

lights are mis-ty in the ri-ver. In the dark-ness the trees are full of

144

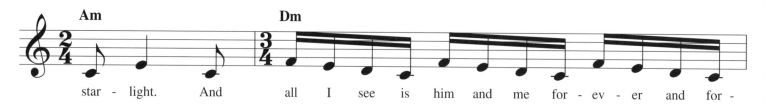

star - light. And all I see is him and me for - ev - er and for -

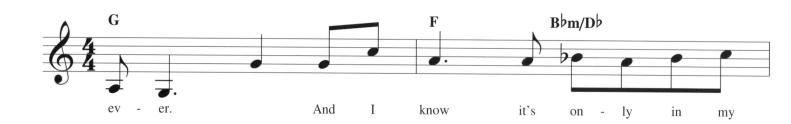

ev - er. And I know it's on - ly in my

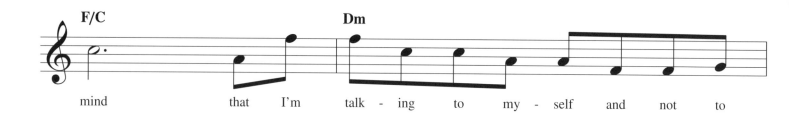

mind that I'm talk - ing to my - self and not to

him. And al - though I know that he is

blind, still I say there's a way for us. I

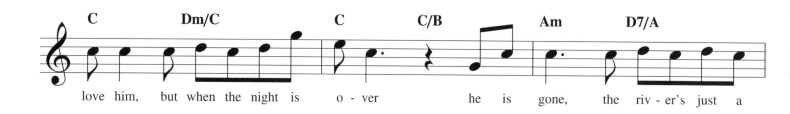

love him, but when the night is o - ver he is gone, the riv - er's just a

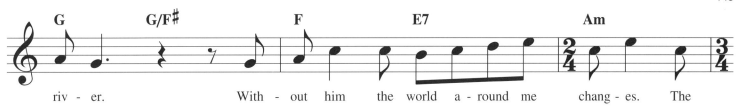

riv - er. With - out him the world a - round me chang - es. The

trees are bare and ev - 'ry - where the streets are full of stran - gers. I

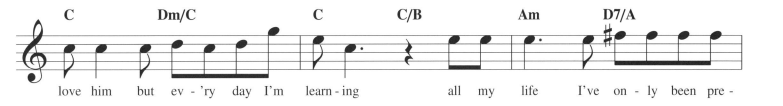

love him but ev - 'ry day I'm learn - ing all my life I've on - ly been pre -

tend - ing. With - out me his world will go on turn - ing. The

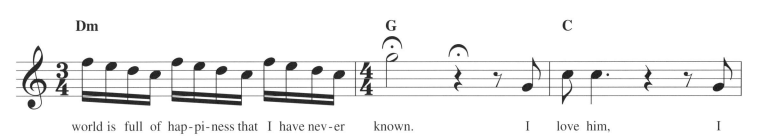

world is full of hap - pi - ness that I have nev - er known. I love him, I

love him, I love him, but on - ly on my own.

MY DARLING, MY DARLING
from WHERE'S CHARLEY?

By FRANK LOESSER

Moderately

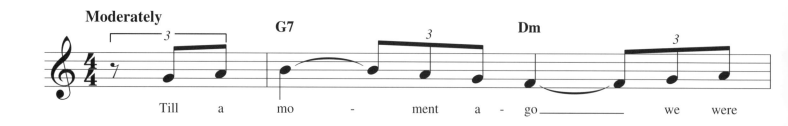

Till a mo - ment a - go _____ we were

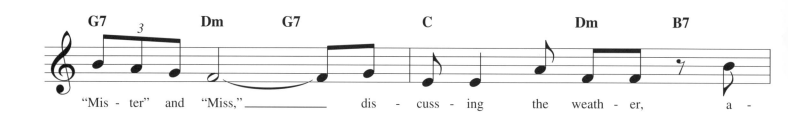

"Mis - ter" and "Miss," _____ dis - cuss - ing the weath - er, a -

void - ing each oth - er's eye. _____ Till a mo - ment a - go _____ when we

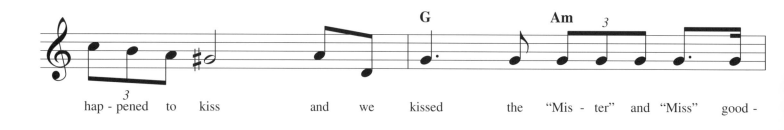

hap - pened to kiss and we kissed the "Mis - ter" and "Miss" good -

bye. Now at last I can sigh. My

Slow, with a beat

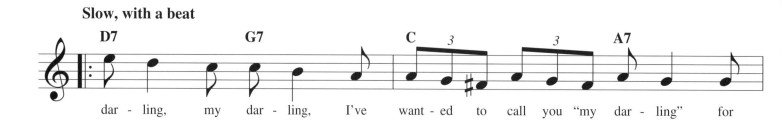

dar - ling, my dar - ling, I've want - ed to call you "my dar - ling" for

man - y and man - y a day. My

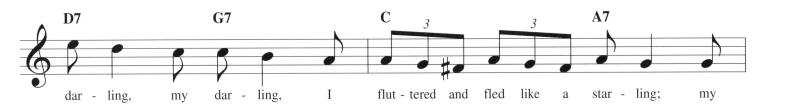

dar - ling, my dar - ling, I flut - tered and fled like a star - ling; my

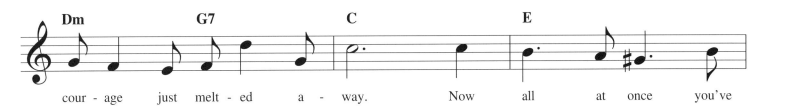

cour - age just melt - ed a - way. Now all at once you've

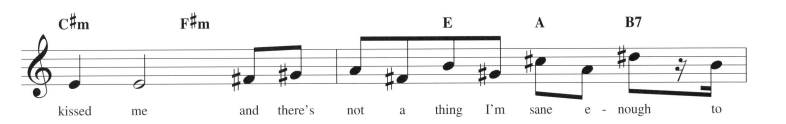

kissed me and there's not a thing I'm sane e - nough to

say_____ ex - cept my dar - ling, my dar - ling, get

used to that name of "my dar - ling," it's here to

stay._____ My stay.

MY SHIP
from the Musical Production LADY IN THE DARK

Words by IRA GERSHWIN
Music by KURT WEILL

Moderately slow

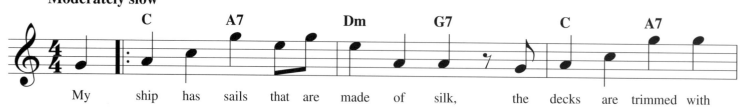

My ship has sails that are made of silk, the decks are trimmed with

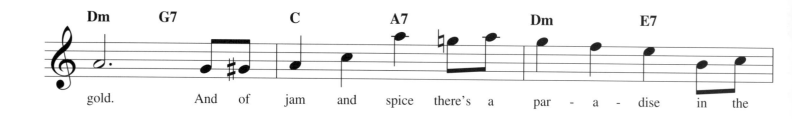

gold. And of jam and spice there's a par - a - dise in the

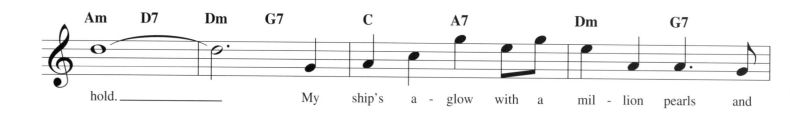

hold._____ My ship's a - glow with a mil - lion pearls and

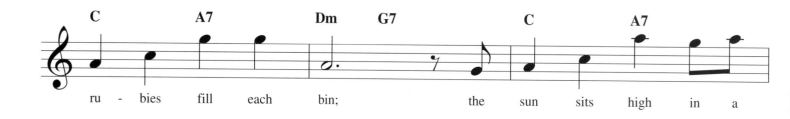

ru - bies fill each bin; the sun sits high in a

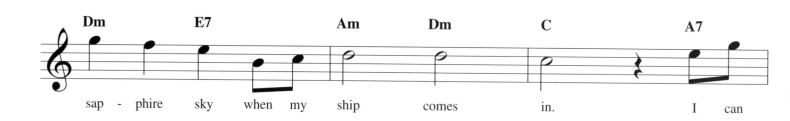

sap - phire sky when my ship comes in. I can

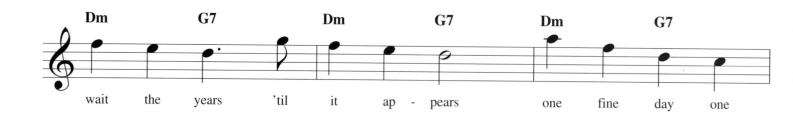

wait the years 'til it ap - pears one fine day one

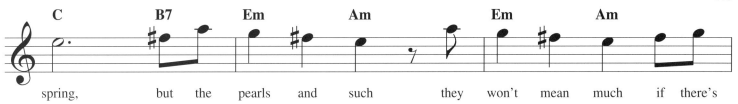
spring, but the pearls and such they won't mean much if there's

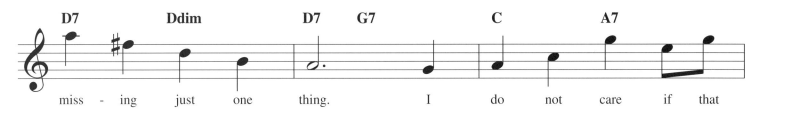
miss - ing just one thing. I do not care if that

day ar - rives, that dream need nev - er be, if the

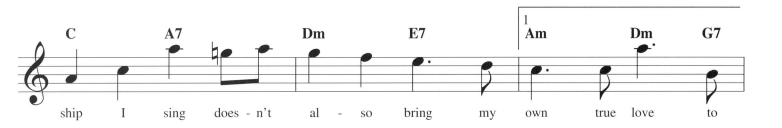
ship I sing does - n't al - so bring my own true love to

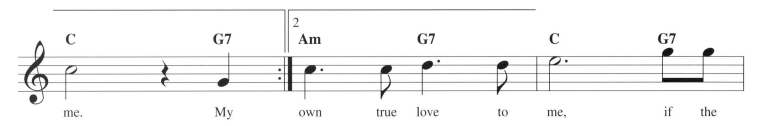
me. My own true love to me, if the

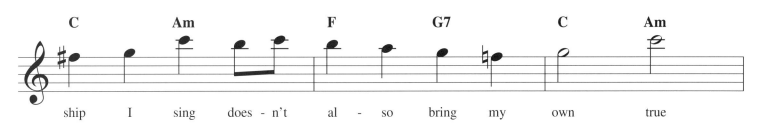
ship I sing does - n't al - so bring my own true

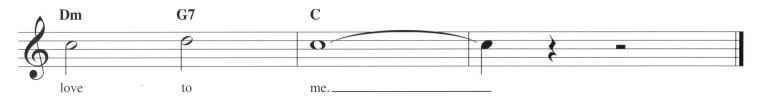
love to me.

OL' MAN RIVER
from SHOW BOAT

Lyrics by OSCAR HAMMERSTEIN II
Music by JEROME KERN

Slowly

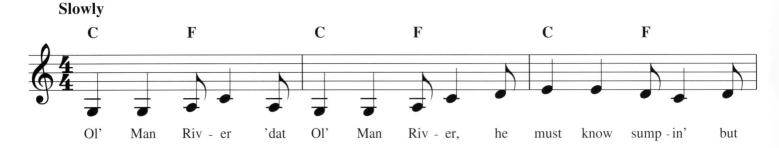

Ol' Man Riv - er 'dat Ol' Man Riv - er, he must know sump - in' but

don't say noth - in'. He jus' keeps roll - in', he keeps on roll - in' a -

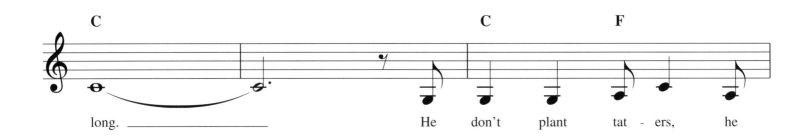

long. _____ He don't plant tat - ers, he

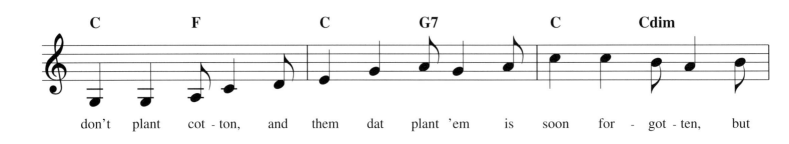

don't plant cot - ton, and them dat plant 'em is soon for - got - ten, but

Ol' Man Riv - er, he just keeps roll - in' a - long. _____

151

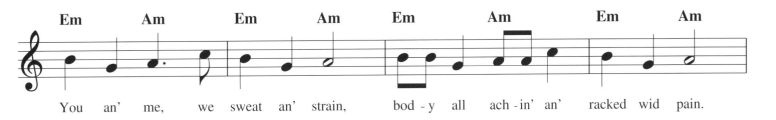

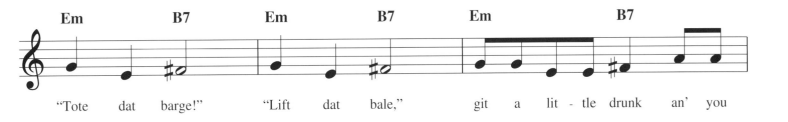

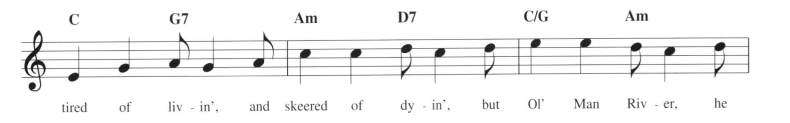

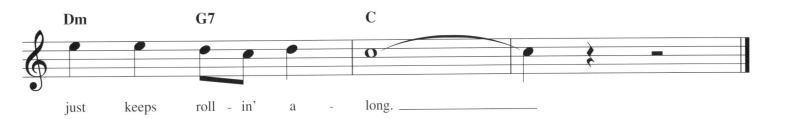

ONCE IN A LIFETIME
from the Musical Production STOP THE WORLD – I WANT TO GET OFF

Words and Music by LESLIE BRICUSSE
and ANTHONY NEWLEY

THE OTHER SIDE OF THE TRACKS
from LITTLE ME

Music by CY COLEMAN
Lyrics by CAROLYN LEIGH

Deliberate tempo, intense and driving

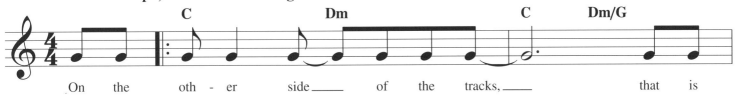

On the oth - er side ___ of the tracks, ___ that is

where I'm go - in' to be. ___ On the oth - er side ___ of that

great di - vide, ___ be - tween fame and for - tune and me! Gon - na

put my shad - ows be - hind me, ___ give my in - hi - bi - tions the

axe, and to - mor - row morn - ing you'll find me on the

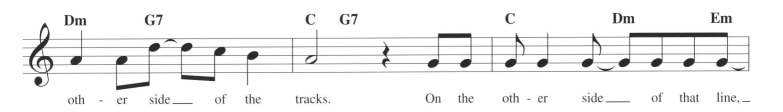

oth - er side ___ of the tracks. On the oth - er side ___ of that line, ___

___ where the life is fan - cy and free, ___ gon - na

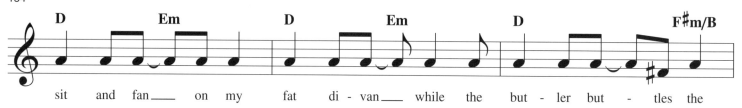

sit and fan___ on my fat di - van___ while the but - ler but - tles the

tea! But for now I'm fac - in' the fenc - es, and I

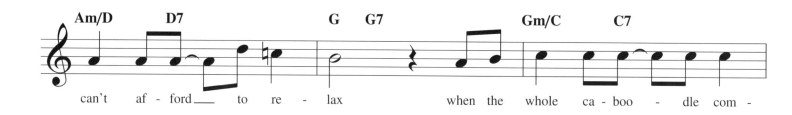

can't af - ford___ to re - lax when the whole ca - boo - dle com -

menc - es on the oth - er side___ of the tracks. So I'm

off and run - nin' o - ver the rail. I'm goin' gun - nin' af -

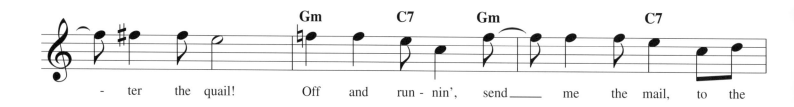

- ter the quail! Off and run - nin', send___ me the mail, to the

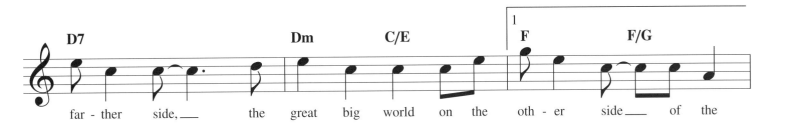

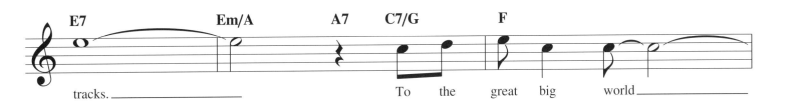

ONCE IN LOVE WITH AMY
from WHERE'S CHARLEY?

By FRANK LOESSER

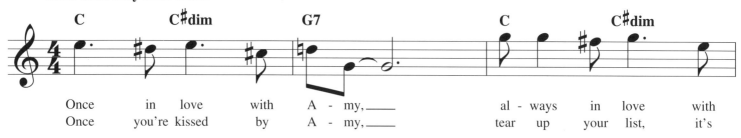

Once in love with A - my,_____ al - ways in love with
Once you're kissed by A - my,_____ tear up your list, it's

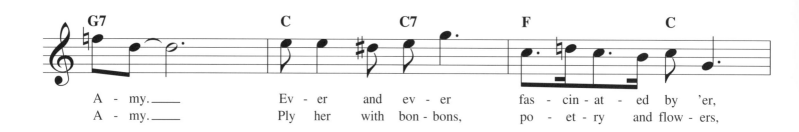

A - my._____ Ev - er and ev - er fas - cin - at - ed by 'er,
A - my._____ Ply her with bon - bons, po - et - ry and flow - ers,

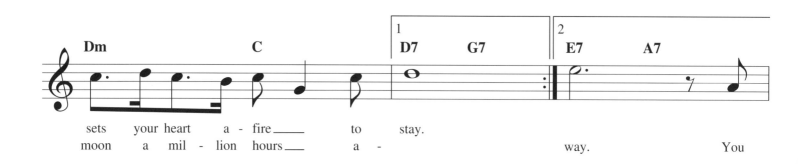

sets your heart a - fire_____ to stay.
moon a mil - lion hours_____ a - way. You

might be quite the fick - le - heart - ed ro - ver, so

care - free and bold who loves a girl and lat - er thinks it

157

o - ver and just quits cold. But

once in love with A - my,_____ al - ways in love with

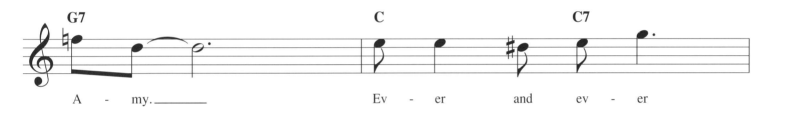

A - my._____ Ev - er and ev - er

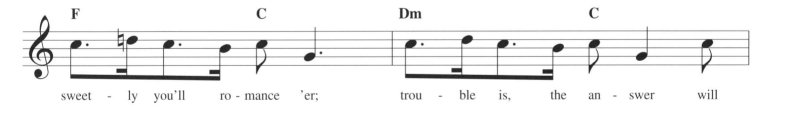

sweet - ly you'll ro - mance 'er; trou - ble is, the an - swer will

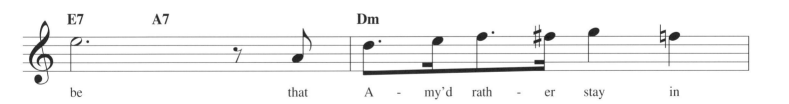

be that A - my'd rath - er stay in

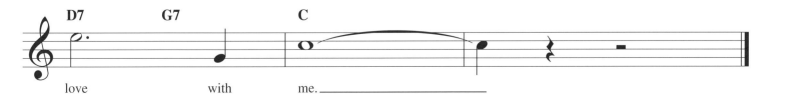

love with me._____

THE PARTY'S OVER
from BELLS ARE RINGING

Words by BETTY COMDEN and ADOLPH GREEN
Music by JULE STYNE

Moderately slow

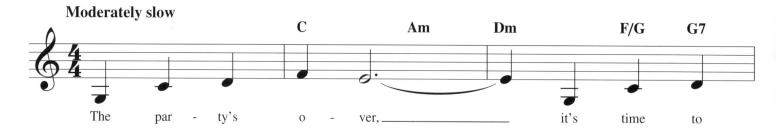

The par - ty's o - ver, _____ it's time to

call it a day. _____ They've burst your pret - ty bal - loon and

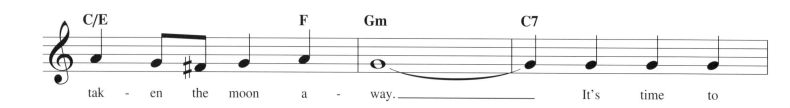

tak - en the moon a - way. _____ It's time to

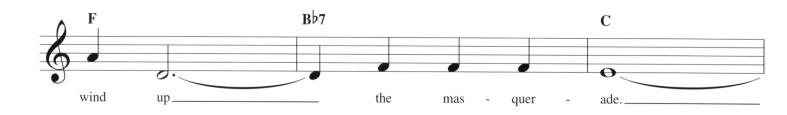

wind up _____ the mas - quer - ade. _____

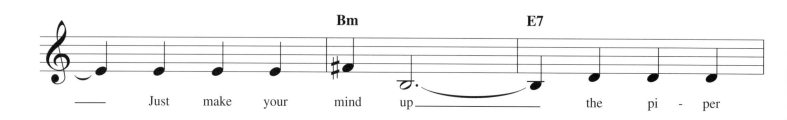

_____ Just make your mind up _____ the pi - per

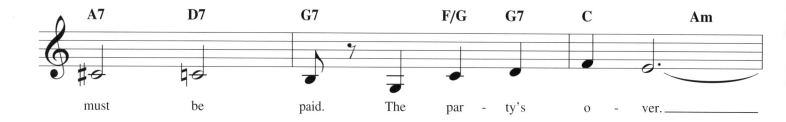

must be paid. The par - ty's o - ver. _____

Dm   F/G   G7   C   Am   Dm   F/G   G7

_____ The can - dles flick - er and dim. _____ You danced and

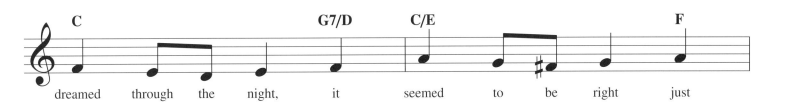

C   G7/D   C/E   F

dreamed through the night, it seemed to be right just

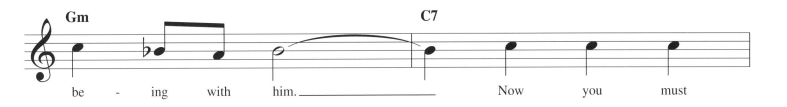

Gm   C7

be - ing with him. _____ Now you must

F   G7   Gm/E

wake up, _____ all dreams must end. _____

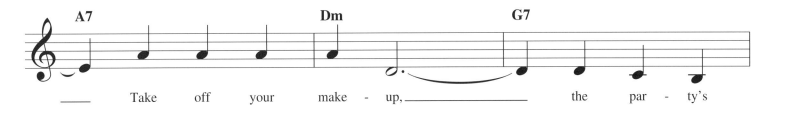

A7   Dm   G7

_____ Take off your make - up, _____ the par - ty's

C   Am   Dm

o - ver. _____ It's all o - ver _____

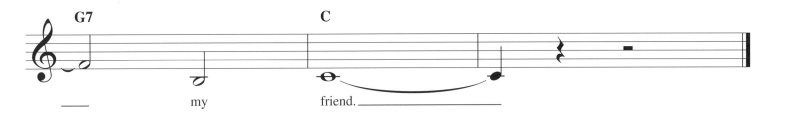

G7   C

_____ my friend. _____

THE PHANTOM OF THE OPERA
from THE PHANTOM OF THE OPERA

Music by ANDREW LLOYD WEBBER
Lyrics by CHARLES HART
Additional Lyrics by RICHARD STILGOE and MIKE BATT

Moderately fast

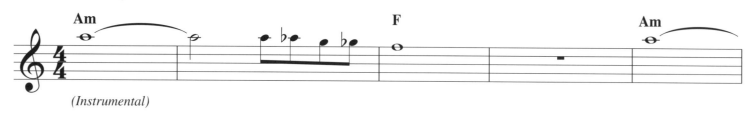

(Instrumental)

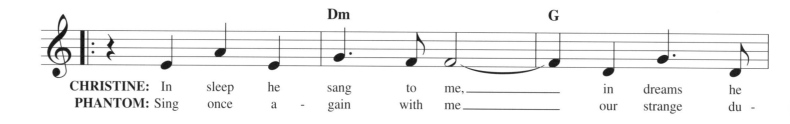

CHRISTINE: In sleep he sang to me, in dreams he

PHANTOM: Sing once a - gain with me our strange du -

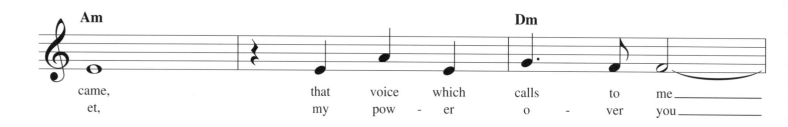

came, that voice which calls to me

et, my pow - er o - ver you

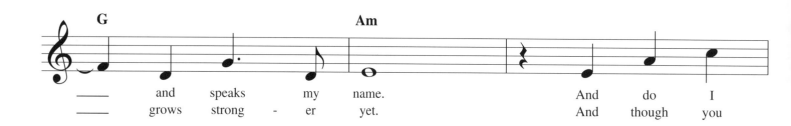

and speaks my name. And do I

grows strong - er yet. And though you

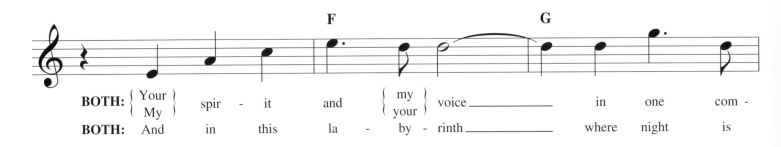

BOTH: { Your / My } spir - it and { my / your } voice _____ in one com -

BOTH: And in this la - by - rinth _____ where night is

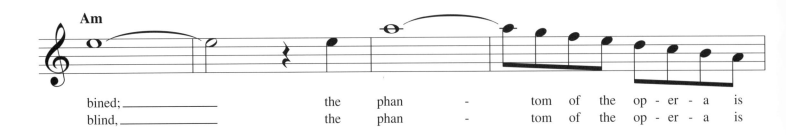

bined; _____ the phan - tom of the op - er - a is

blind, _____ the phan - tom of the op - er - a is

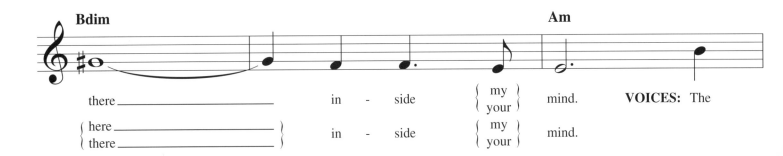

there _____ in - side { my / your } mind. **VOICES:** The

{ here _____ / there _____ } in - side { my / your } mind.

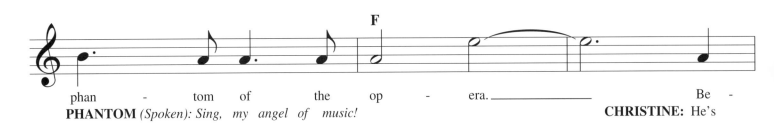

phan - tom of the op - era. _____ Be -

PHANTOM *(Spoken): Sing, my angel of music!* **CHRISTINE:** He's

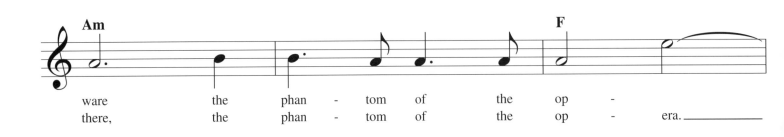

ware the phan - tom of the op -

there, the phan - tom of the op - era. _____

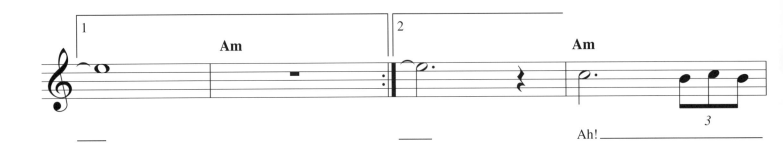

_____ _____

Ah! _____

PHANTOM: *Sing, my angel, sing!*

Ah!

PHANTOM *(1st time):* Sing, for me!

Ah!

PHANTOM: *Sing, my angel of music!*

Ah!   Ah!

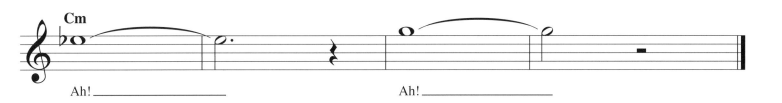

Ah!   Ah!

POPULAR
from the Broadway Musical WICKED

Music and Lyrics by
STEPHEN SCHWARTZ

Sweetly

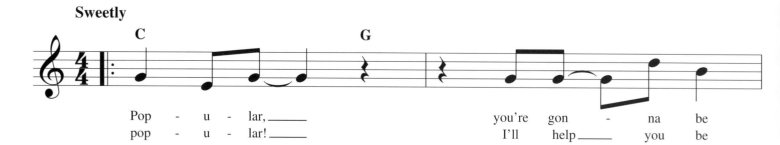

Pop - u - lar,_____ you're gon - na be
pop - u - lar!_____ I'll help_____ you be

pop - u - lar! I'll teach you the prop - er ploys when you
pop - u - lar! You'll hang with the right co - horts, you'll be

talk to boys, lit - tle ways to flirt and flounce. I'll show you what
good at sports, know the slang you've got to

shoes to wear, how to fix your hair,_____ ev - 'ry - thing that

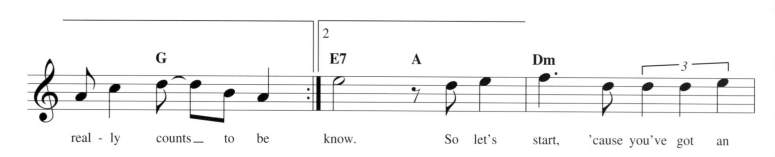

real - ly counts_____ to be know. So let's start, 'cause you've got an

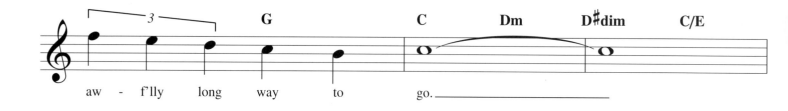

aw - f'lly long way to go._____

Don't be of - fend - ed by my frank an - al - y - sis,

think of it as per - son - al - i - ty di - al - y - sis.

Now that I've chos - en to be - come a pal,___ a sis -

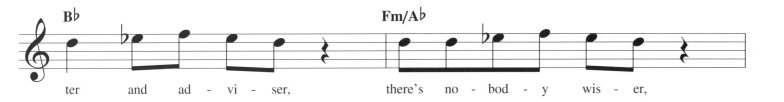

ter and ad - vi - ser, there's no - bod - y wis - er,

not when it comes___ to pop - u - lar.___ I know___ a - bout

pop - u - lar! And with an as - sist from me to be

who you'll be, in - stead of drear - y who - you - were... are... There's

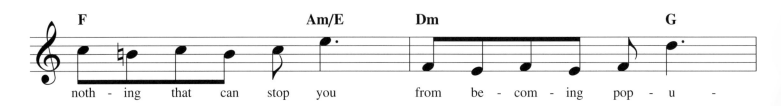

noth - ing that can stop you from be - com - ing pop - u -

lar... lar..._____ La la_____ la la___

____ We're gon - na make you pop - u -

lar!_____ When I see de - press - ing crea - tures

with un - pre - pos - sess - ing fea - tures, I re - mind them

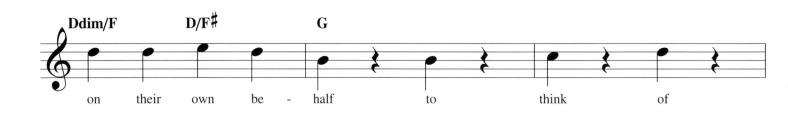

on their own be - half to think of

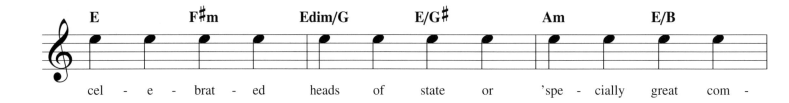

cel - e - brat - ed heads of state or 'spe - cially great com -

mu - ni - ca - tors... Did they have brains or knowl - edge?

Don't make me laugh! *(Instrumental)* They were pop - u - lar___ *Please!*

It's all___ a - bout pop - u - lar! It's not a - bout

ap - ti - tude, it's the way you're viewed, so it's ver - y shrewd to

be *(Instrumental)* ver - y, ver - y pop - u - lar like

me! *(Instrumental)* And though you pro - test___ your dis -

168

in - ter - est,____ I know clan - des - tine - ly____ you're

A tempo

gon - na grin and bear it your new - found pop - u - lar - i -

ty.____ La la____

la____ la. You'll be pop - u - lar, just not

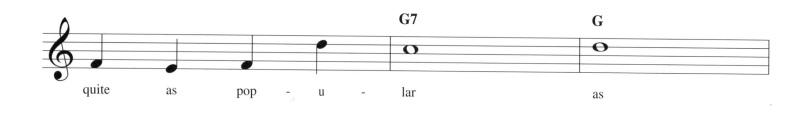

quite as pop - u - lar as

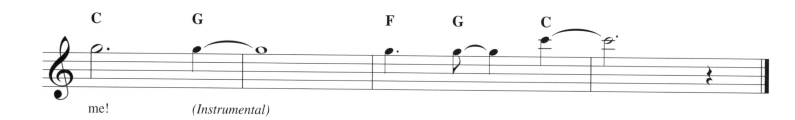

me! *(Instrumental)*

SO IN LOVE
from KISS ME, KATE

Words and Music by
COLE PORTER

Moderately

Strange, dear, but true, dear, when

I'm close to you, dear, the

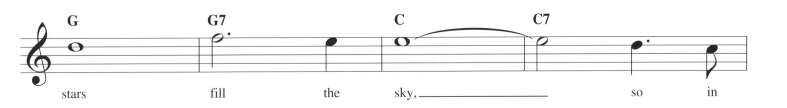

stars fill the sky, so in

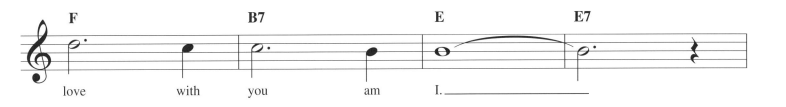

love with you am I.

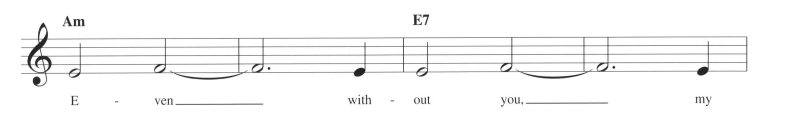

E - ven with - out you, my

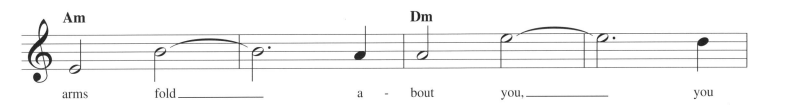

arms fold a - bout you, you

know, dar - ling, why, _____ so in

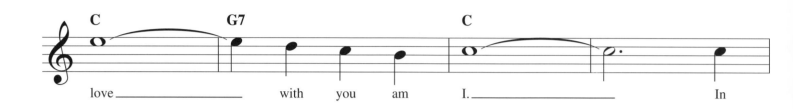

love _____ with you am I. _____ In

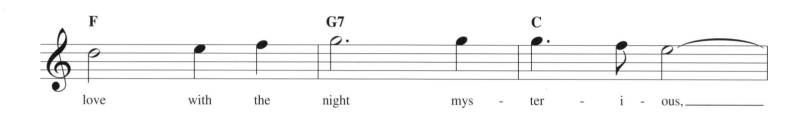

love with the night mys - ter - i - ous, _____

_____ the night when you first were

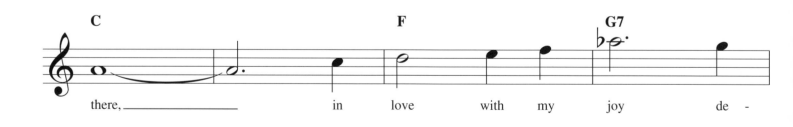

there, _____ in love with my joy de -

lir - i - ous _____ when I knew that you could

care._____ So taunt me_____ and

hurt me,_____ de - ceive me,_____ de -

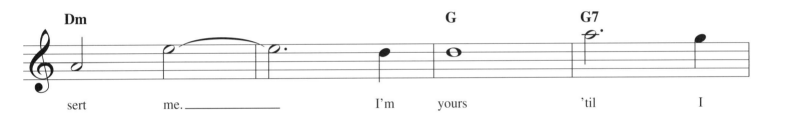

sert me._____ I'm yours 'til I

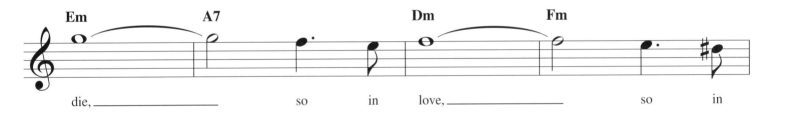

die,_____ so in love,_____ so in

love,_____ so in love with you, my

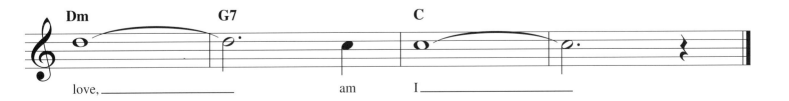

love,_____ am I_____

A PRETTY GIRL IS LIKE A MELODY
from the 1919 Stage Production ZIEGFELD FOLLIES

Words and Music by
IRVING BERLIN

Moderately

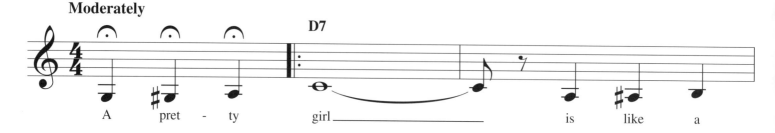

A pret - ty girl _____ is like a

mel - o - dy _____ that haunts you

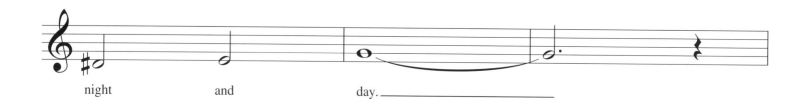

night and day. _____

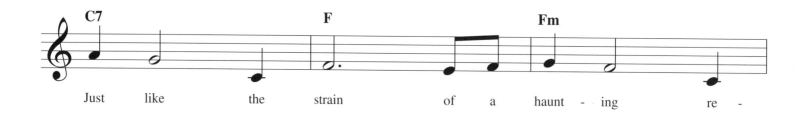

Just like the strain of a haunt - ing re -

frain, she'll start up - on a mar - a - thon and

173

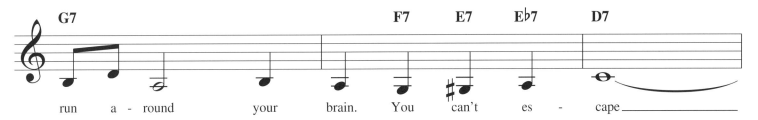

run a - round your brain. You can't es - cape_____

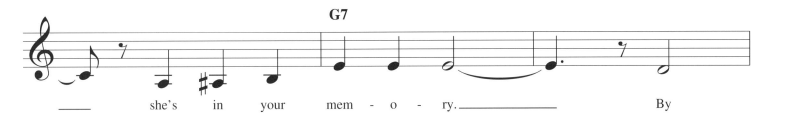

_____ she's in your mem - o - ry._____ By

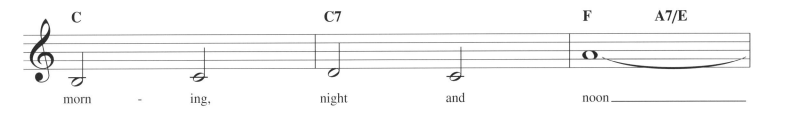

morn - ing, night and noon_____

____ she will leave you and then

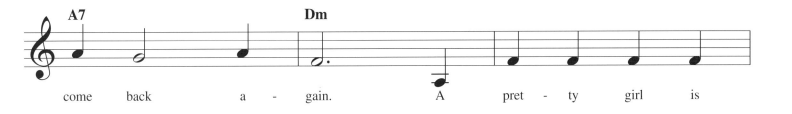

come back a - gain. A pret - ty girl is

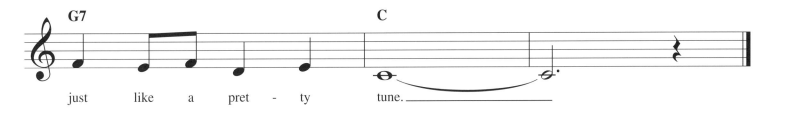

just like a pret - ty tune._____

PUT ON A HAPPY FACE
from BYE BYE BIRDIE

Lyric by LEE ADAMS
Music by CHARLES STROUSE

Lightly

Gray skies are gon - na clear up, _____ put on a hap - py

face. Brush off the clouds and cheer up, _____

put on a hap - py face. Take off the gloom - y

mask of trag - e - dy, it's not your

style. You'll look so good that you'll be glad __ ya' de -

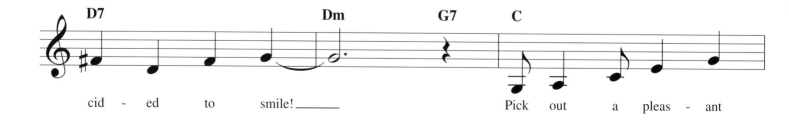

cid - ed to smile! _____ Pick out a pleas - ant

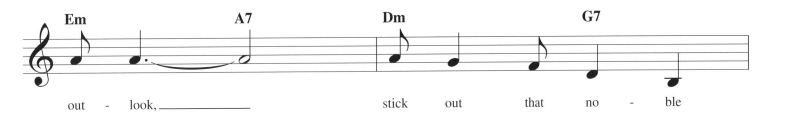

out - look,_____ stick out that no - ble

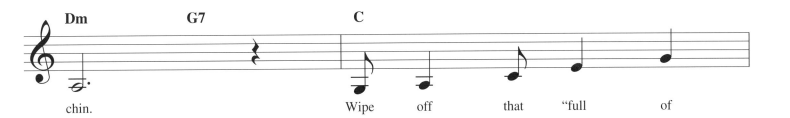

chin. Wipe off that "full of

doubt" look,_____ slap on a hap - py

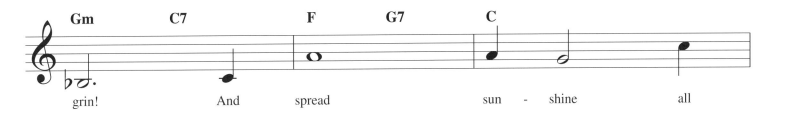

grin! And spread sun - shine all

o - ver the place, just put on a

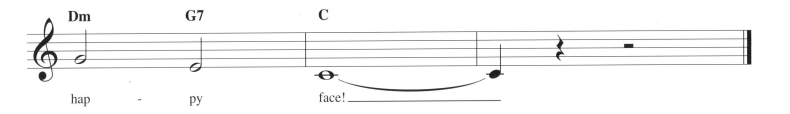

hap - py face!_____

REAL LIVE GIRL
from LITTLE ME

Music by CY COLEMAN
Lyrics by CAROLYN LEIGH

Moderate Waltz

Par - don me, Miss, but I've nev - er done this with a
Noth - ing can beat get - ting swept off your feet by a

real   live   girl. _____
real   live   girl. _____

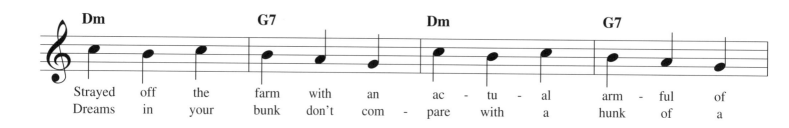

Strayed off the farm with an ac - tu - al arm - ful of
Dreams in your bunk don't com - pare with a hunk of a

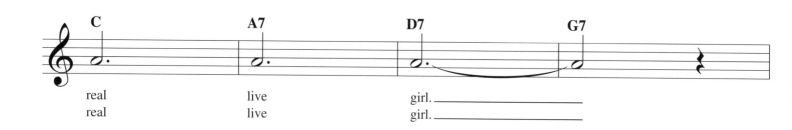

real   live   girl. _____
real   live   girl. _____

Par - don me if your af - fec - tion - ate squeeze
Speak - ing of mir - a - cles, this must be it

177

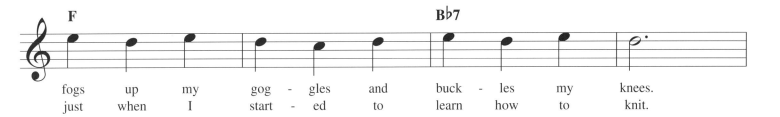

fogs up my gog - gles and buck - les my knees.
just when I start - ed to learn how my to knit.

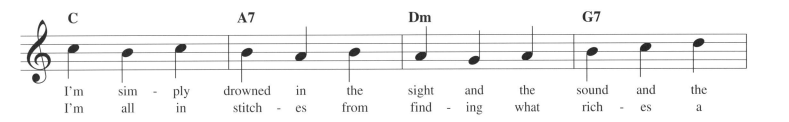

I'm sim - ply drowned in the sight and the sound and the
I'm all in stitch - es from find - ing what rich - es a

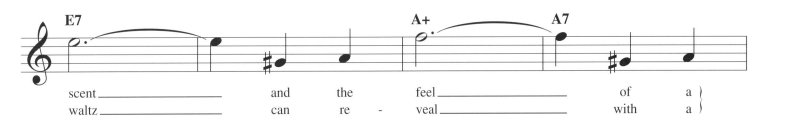

scent_____ and the feel_____ of a
waltz_____ can re - veal_____ with a

real_____ live_____

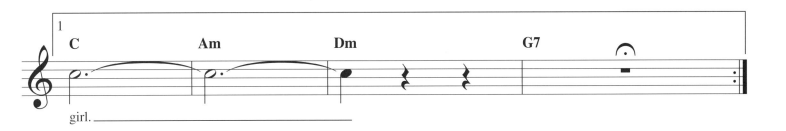

girl._____

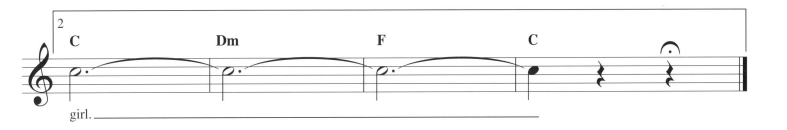

girl._____

SHALL WE DANCE?
from THE KING AND I

Lyrics by OSCAR HAMMERSTEIN II
Music by RICHARD RODGERS

Shall we dance? On a

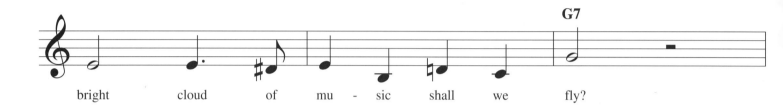

bright cloud of mu - sic shall we fly?

Shall we dance? Shall we

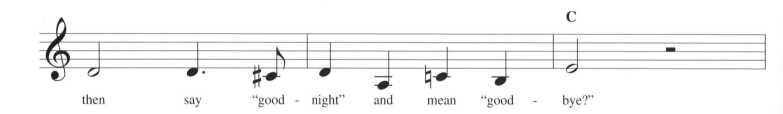

then say "good - night" and mean "good - bye?"

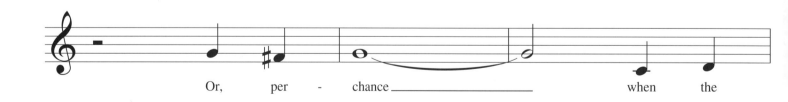

Or, per - chance _____ when the

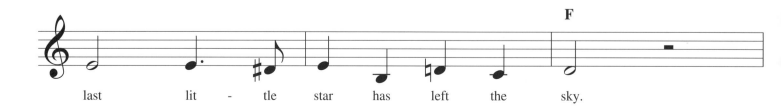

last lit - tle star has left the sky.

Shall we still be to - geth - er with our

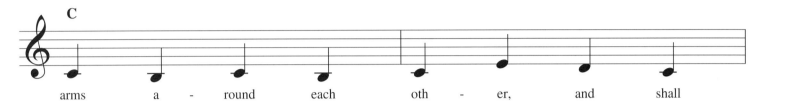

arms a - round each oth - er, and shall

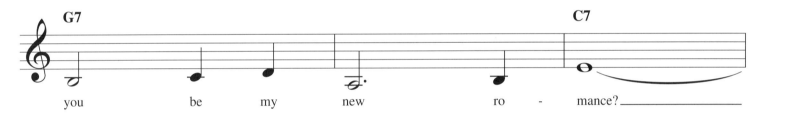

you be my new ro - mance?

On the clear un - der - stand - ing that this

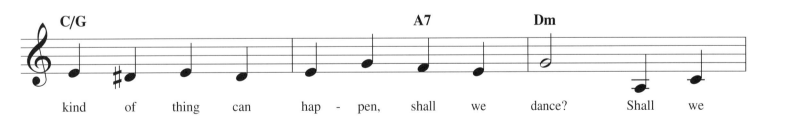

kind of thing can hap - pen, shall we dance? Shall we

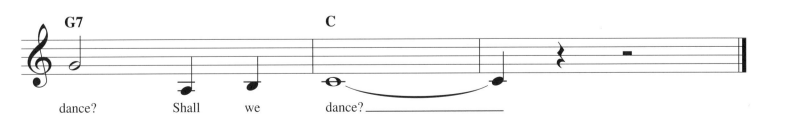

dance? Shall we dance?

SHE LOVES ME
from SHE LOVES ME

Words by SHELDON HARNICK
Music by JERRY BOCK

Moderately bright

A SLEEPIN' BEE
from HOUSE OF FLOWERS

Lyric by TRUMAN CAPOTE and HAROLD ARLEN
Music by HAROLD ARLEN

Moderately

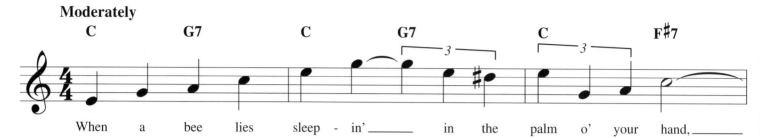

When a bee lies sleep - in' _____ in the palm o' your hand, _____

_____ you're be - witch'd and deep in _____ love's long

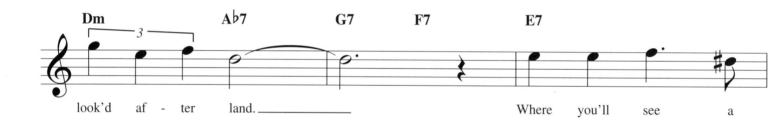

look'd af - ter land. _____ Where you'll see a

sun - up sky with a morn - in' new, and

where the days go laugh - in' by as love comes a - call - in' on

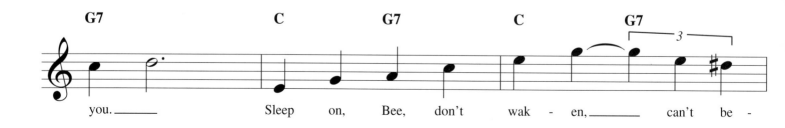

you. _____ Sleep on, Bee, don't wak - en, _____ can't be -

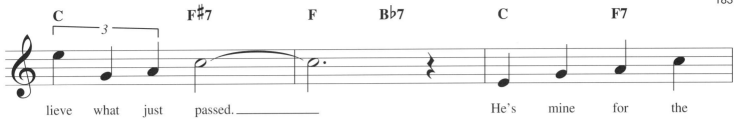

lieve what just passed._____ He's mine for the

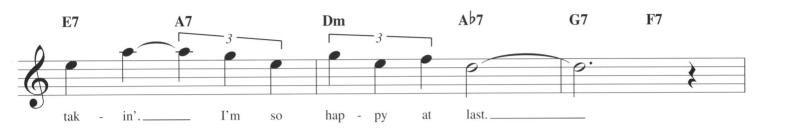

tak - in'._____ I'm so hap - py at last._____

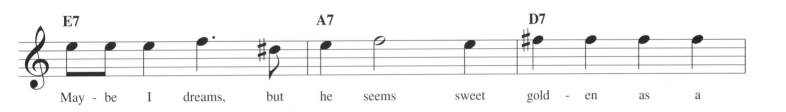

May - be I dreams, but he seems sweet gold - en as a

crown, a sleep - in' bee done told me, I'll

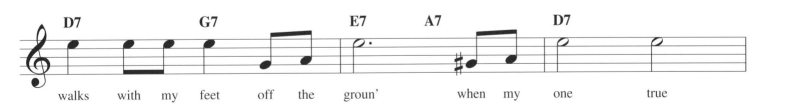

walks with my feet off the groun' when my one true

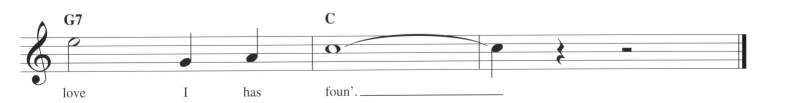

love I has foun'._____

SMALL WORLD
from GYPSY

Words by STEPHEN SONDHEIM
Music by JULE STYNE

185

SOMEONE NICE LIKE YOU

from the Musical Production STOP THE WORLD – I WANT TO GET OFF

Words and Music by LESLIE BRICUSSE
and ANTHONY NEWLEY

Moderately

Why did some-one nice like you, { E - vie, ____
sweet - heart, ____
You ask why did some-one nice like me ____

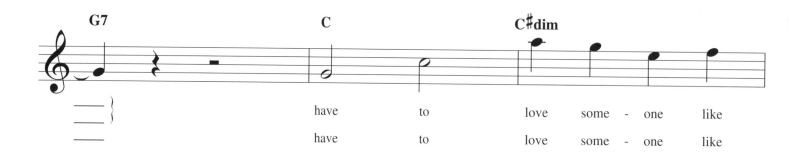

____ } have to love some - one like
____ have to love some - one like

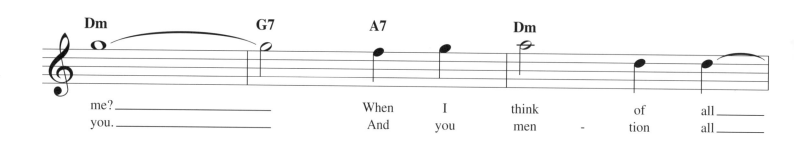

me? ____ When I think of all ____
you. ____ And you men - tion all ____

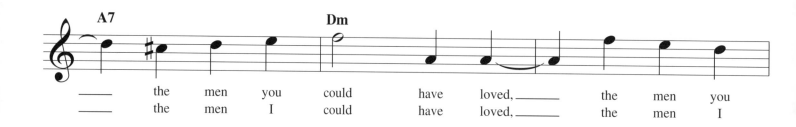

____ the men you could have loved, ____ the men you
____ the men I could have loved, ____ the men I

should have loved ____ who would have loved you. ____
should have loved ____ who would have loved me. ____

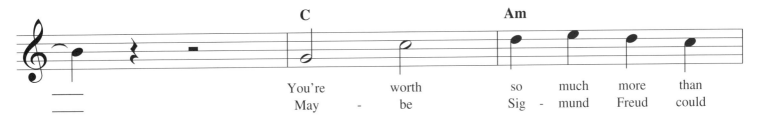

You're   worth   so   much   more   than
May - be   Sig - mund   Freud   could

me,   { E - vie.   }   Be - lieve   you   me,   { E - vie,
   { sweet - heart.   }   { sweet - heart,
tell   you   why   I'll   love   you   till   I   die,

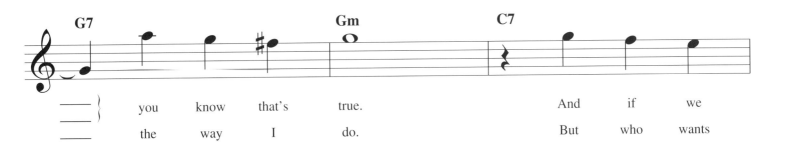

   } you   know   that's   true.   And   if   we
   the   way   I   do.   But   who   wants

could   live   twice,   I'd   make   life   par - a - dise
Freud's   ad - vice?   I'm   sure   it   works   with   mice,

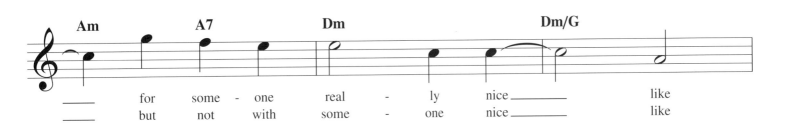

   for   some - one   real - ly   nice   like
   but   not   with   some - one   nice   like

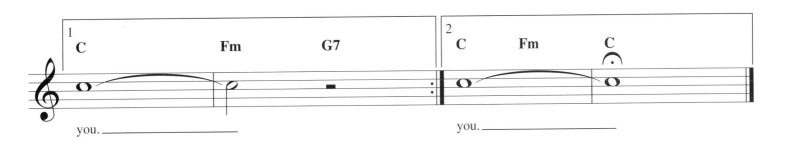

you.   you.

SOMETHING WONDERFUL
from THE KING AND I

Lyrics by OSCAR HAMMERSTEIN II
Music by RICHARD RODGERS

Moderately

He will not al - ways say what you would
The thought - less things he'll do will hurt and

have him say, but, now and then, he'll say
wor - ry you, then all at once he'll do

1. some - thing won - der - ful.
2. some - thing

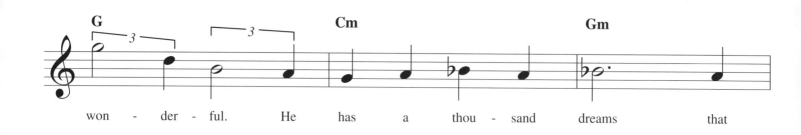

won - der - ful. He has a thou - sand dreams that

won't come true. You know that he be -

189

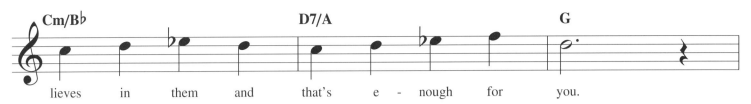

lieves in them and that's e - nough for you.

You'll al - ways go a - long, de - fend him

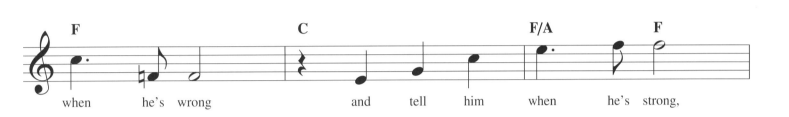

when he's wrong and tell him when he's strong,

he is won - der - ful. He'll al - ways

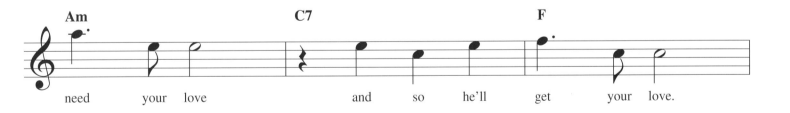

need your love and so he'll get your love.

A man who needs your love can be

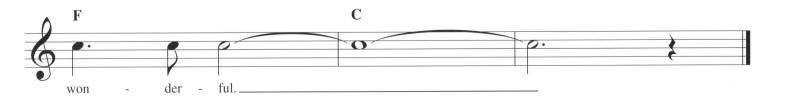

won - der - ful.

THE SONG IS YOU
from MUSIC IN THE AIR

Lyrics by OSCAR HAMMERSTEIN II
Music by JEROME KERN

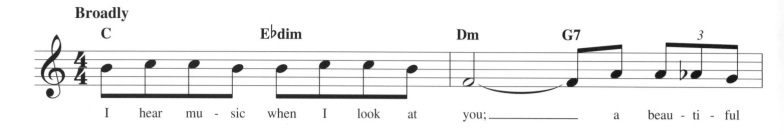

I hear mu - sic when I look at you;_____ a beau - ti - ful

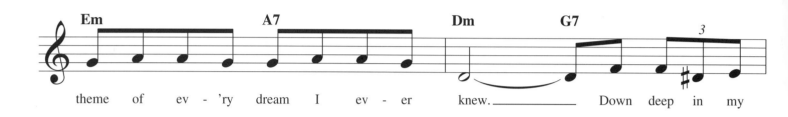

theme of ev - 'ry dream I ev - er knew._____ Down deep in my

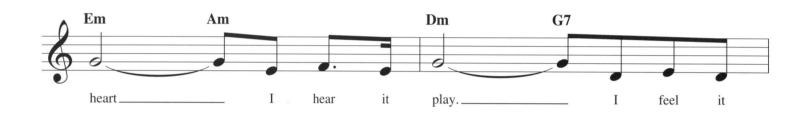

heart_____ I hear it play._____ I feel it

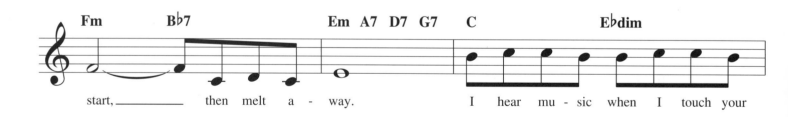

start,_____ then melt a - way. I hear mu - sic when I touch your

hand;_____ a beau - ti - ful mel - o - dy from some en - chant - ed

land._____ Down deep in my heart,_____ I hear it say,_____ is this the

0.02191

SPEAK LOW
from the Musical Production ONE TOUCH OF VENUS

Words by OGDEN NASH
Music by KURT WEILL

Rhumba or Beguine

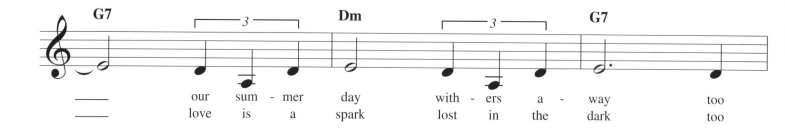

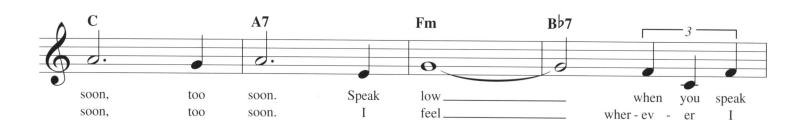

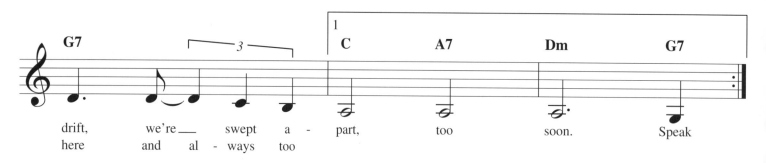

193

love   so   brief.   Love   is   pure   gold____

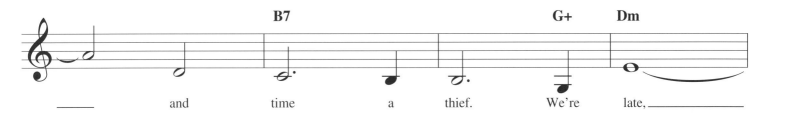
____   and   time   a   thief.   We're   late,____

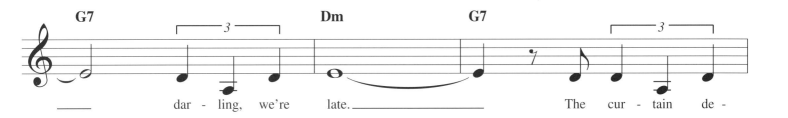
____   dar - ling,   we're   late.____   The   cur - tain   de -

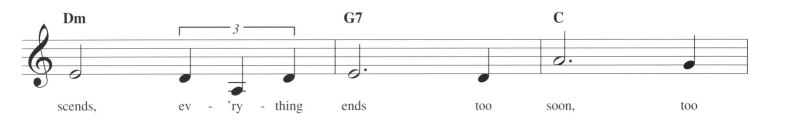
scends,   ev - 'ry - thing   ends   too   soon,   too

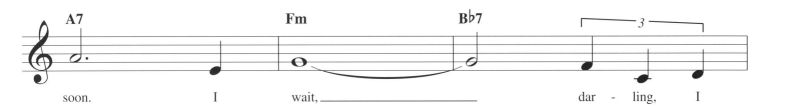
soon.   I   wait,____   dar - ling,   I

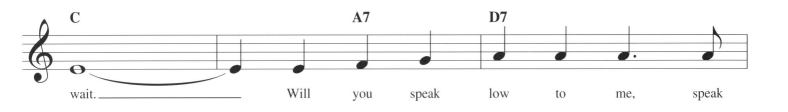
wait.____   Will   you   speak   low   to   me,   speak

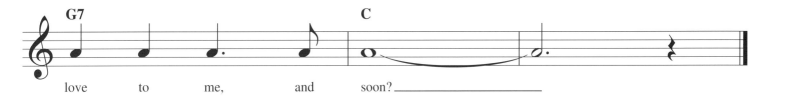
love   to   me,   and   soon?____

STANDING ON THE CORNER

from THE MOST HAPPY FELLA

By FRANK LOESSER

Moderately

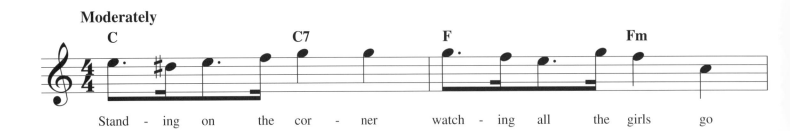

Stand - ing on the cor - ner watch - ing all the girls go

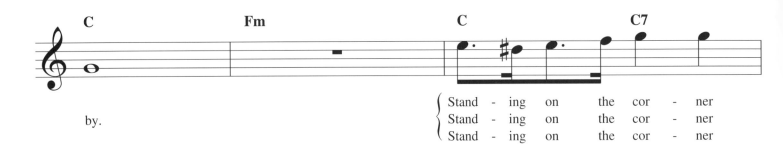

by.

Stand - ing on the cor - ner
Stand - ing on the cor - ner
Stand - ing on the cor - ner

watch - ing all the girls go by.
giv - ing all the girls the eye.
un - der - neath a spring - time sky.

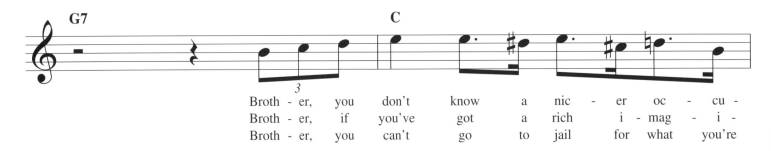

Broth - er, you don't know a nic - er oc - cu -
Broth - er, if you've got a rich i - mag - i -
Broth - er, you can't go to jail for what you're

pa - tion mat - ter of fact nei - ther do
na - tion, give it a whirl, give it a
think - ing, or for the "woooooo" look in your

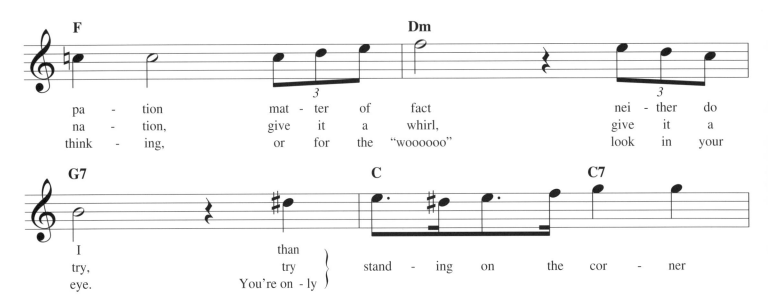

I than
try, try ⎱ stand - ing on the cor - ner
eye. You're on - ly ⎰

195

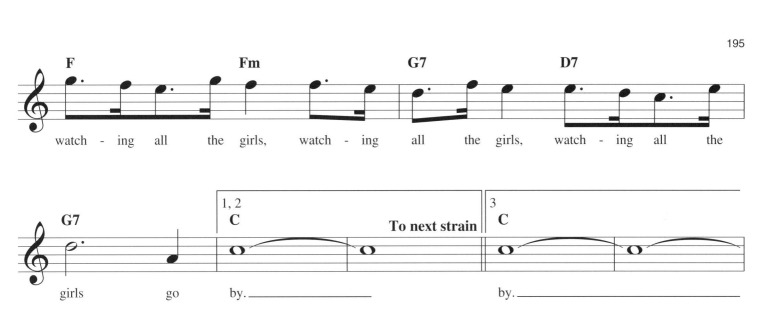

watch - ing all the girls, watch - ing all the girls, watch - ing all the

girls go by. _____ by. _____

_____

I'm the cat that got the cream,
Sat - ur - day and I'm so broke,

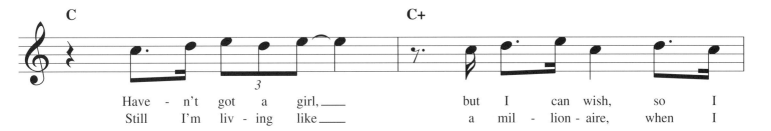

have - n't got a girl,____ but I can dream.
could - n't buy a girl____ a nick - el coke.

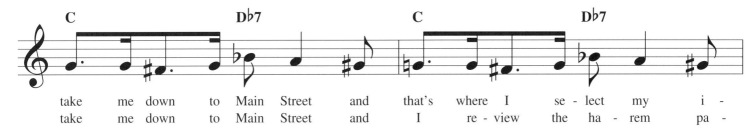

Have - n't got a girl,____ but I can wish, so I
Still I'm liv - ing like____ a mil - lion - aire, when I

take me down to Main Street and that's where I se - lect my i -
take me down to Main Street and I re - view the ha - rem pa -

mag - i - na - ry dish!
rad - ing for me there!

STRANGER IN PARADISE
from KISMET

Words and Music by ROBERT WRIGHT
and GEORGE FORREST
(Music Based on Themes of A. Borodin)

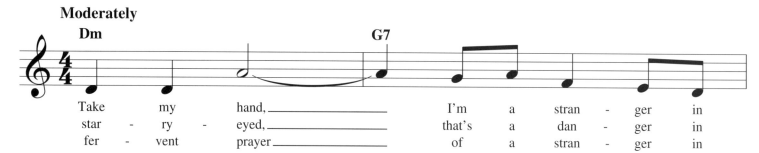

Take my hand, _____ I'm a stran-ger in
star-ry-eyed, _____ that's a dan-ger in
fer-vent prayer _____ of a stran-ger in

par-a-dise, all lost in a won-der-land, _____
par-a-dise for mor-tals who stand be-side _____
par-a-dise? Don't send me in dark de-spair _____

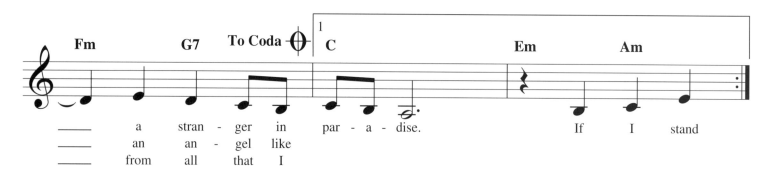

_____ a stran-ger in par-a-dise. If I stand
_____ an an-gel like
_____ from all that I

you. I saw your face _____

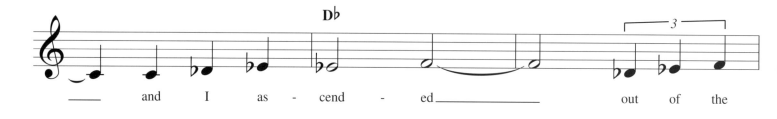

_____ and I as-cend-ed _____ out of the

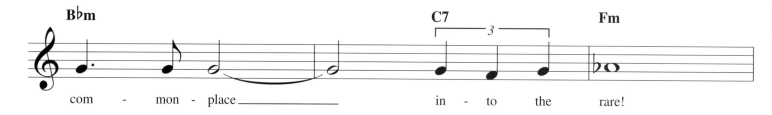

com-mon-place _____ in-to the rare!

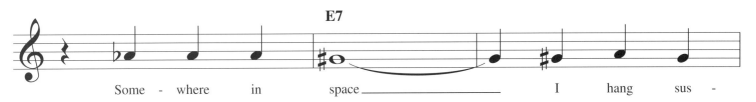

Some - where in space _____ I hang sus -

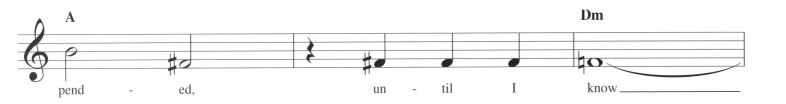

pend - ed, un - til I know _____

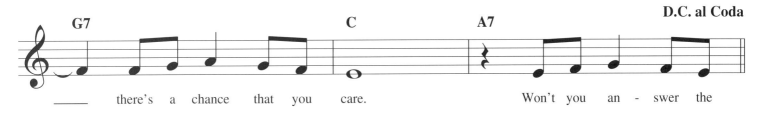

____ there's a chance that you care. Won't you an - swer the

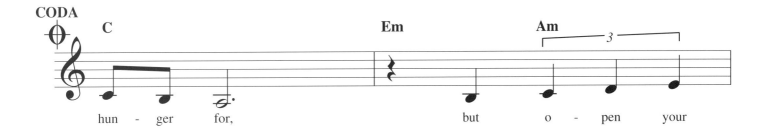

hun - ger for, but o - pen your

an - gel's arms _____ to the stran - ger in

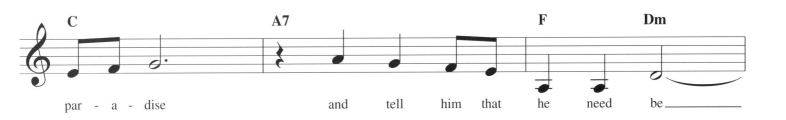

par - a - dise and tell him that he need be _____

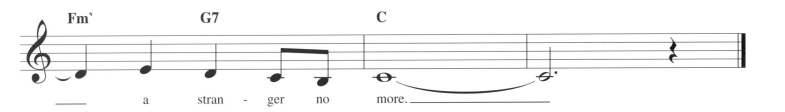

____ a stran - ger no more. _____

SUNRISE, SUNSET
from the Musical FIDDLER ON THE ROOF

Words by SHELDON HARNICK
Music by JERRY BOCK

THE SWEETEST SOUNDS
from NO STRINGS

Lyrics and Music by
RICHARD RODGERS

WHAT'LL I DO?

from MUSIC BOX REVUE OF 1924

Words and Music by
IRVING BERLIN

Moderate Waltz

What -'ll I do _____ when you _____ are far _____ a -
do _____ when I _____ am won - d'ring

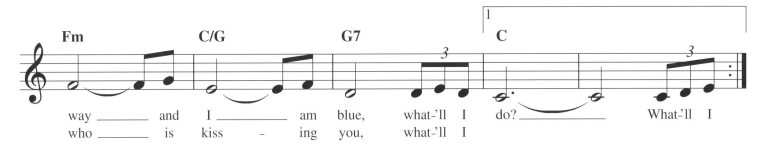

way _____ and I _____ am blue, what'll I do? _____ What'll I
who _____ is kiss - ing you, what'll I

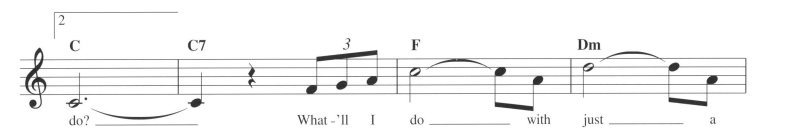

do? _____ What -'ll I do _____ with just _____ a

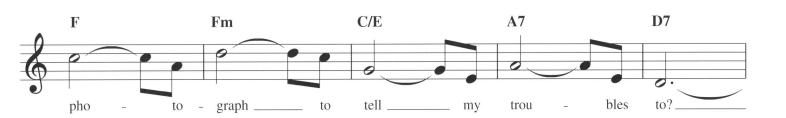

pho - to - graph _____ to tell _____ my trou - bles to? _____

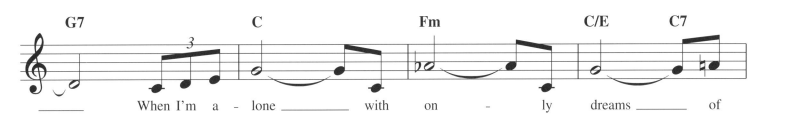

_____ When I'm a - lone _____ with on - ly dreams _____ of

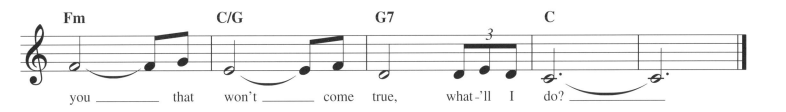

you _____ that won't _____ come true, what -'ll I do? _____

TELL ME ON A SUNDAY
from SONG & DANCE

Music by ANDREW LLOYD WEBBER
Lyrics by DON BLACK

Slowly

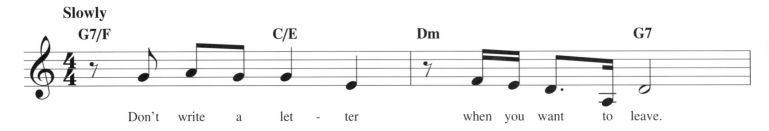

Don't write a let - ter when you want to leave.

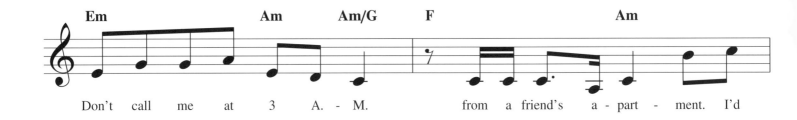

Don't call me at 3 A. - M. from a friend's a - part - ment. I'd

like to choose how I hear the news. Take me

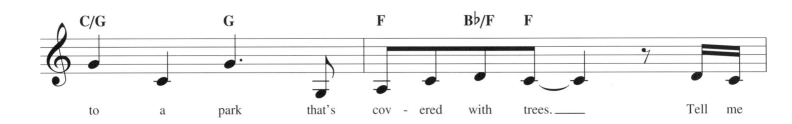

to a park that's cov - ered with trees. Tell me

on a Sun - day please. Let me down eas - y,

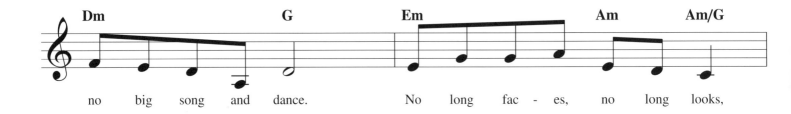

no big song and dance. No long fac - es, no long looks,

no deep con - ver - sa - tion.___ I know the way we should

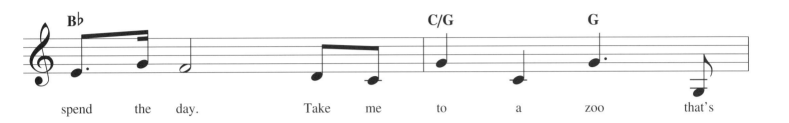

spend the day. Take me to a zoo that's

got chim - pan - zees.___ Tell me on a Sun - day

please.___ Don't want to know who's to blame,

it won't help know - ing. Don't want to fight day and night,

bad e - nough___ you're go - ing. Don't leave in si - lence

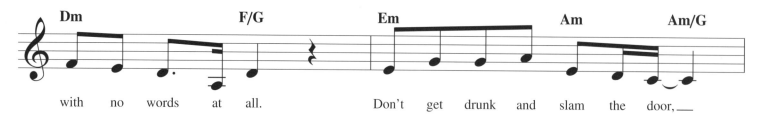

with no words at all. Don't get drunk and slam the door,___

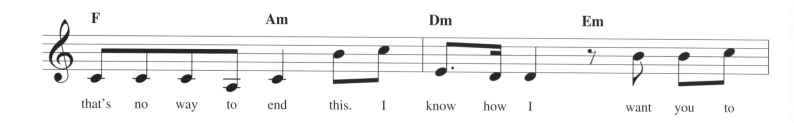

that's no way to end this. I know how I want you to

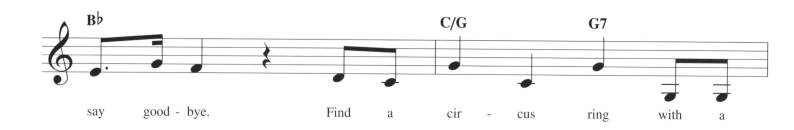

say good - bye. Find a cir - cus ring with a

fly - ing trap - eze._____ Tell me on a Sun - day

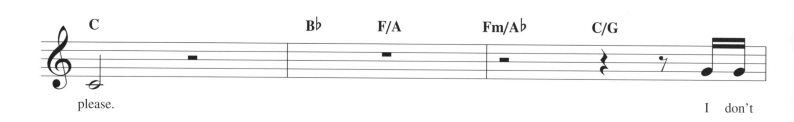

please. I don't

want to fight day and night, bad e - nough you're go - ing.

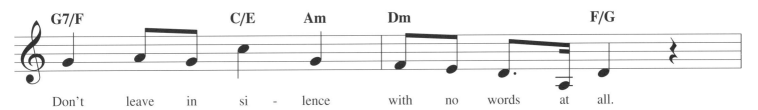

Don't leave in si - lence with no words at all.

Don't get drunk and slam the door, that's no way to end this. I

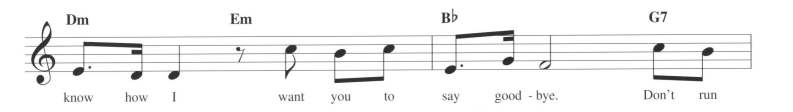

know how I want you to say good - bye. Don't run

off in the pour - ing rain. Don't call me as they call your plane. Take the

hurt out of all the pain. Take me to a park that's

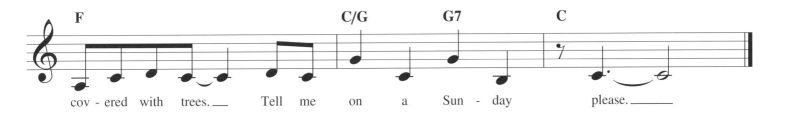

cov - ered with trees. ___ Tell me on a Sun - day please. ___

THANK HEAVEN FOR LITTLE GIRLS
from GIGI

Words by ALAN JAY LERNER
Music by FREDERICK LOEWE

Moderately

Thank heav - en _____ for lit - tle girls! _____

_____ For lit - tle girls get big - ger ev - 'ry

day. _____ Thank heav - en _____

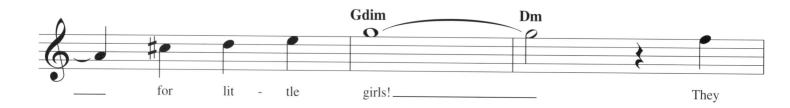

_____ for lit - tle girls! _____ They

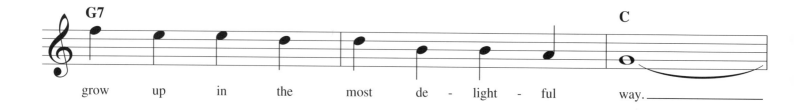

grow up in the most de - light - ful way. _____

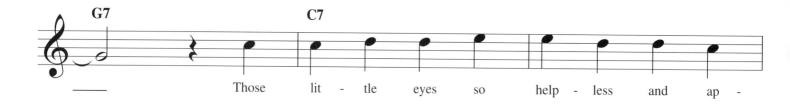

_____ Those lit - tle eyes so help - less and ap -

peal - ing _____ one day will flash and send you

crash - ing through the ceil - ing._____ Thank

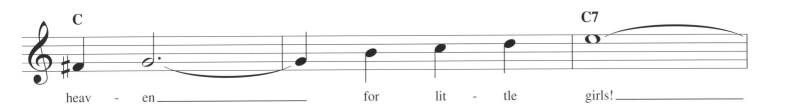

heav - en _____ for lit - tle girls! _____

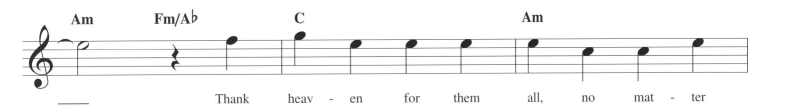

____ Thank heav - en for them all, no mat - ter

where, no mat - ter who. With - out them what would

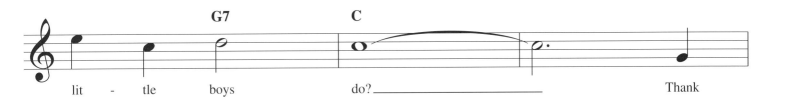

lit - tle boys do? _____ Thank

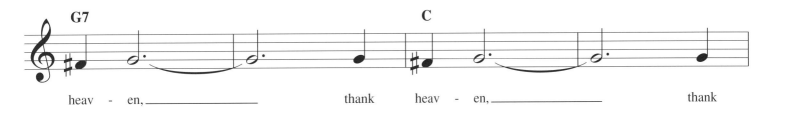

heav - en, _____ thank heav - en, _____ thank

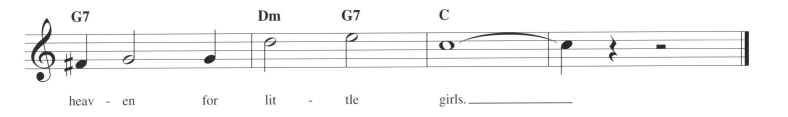

heav - en for lit - tle girls. _____

THIS NEARLY WAS MINE
from SOUTH PACIFIC

Lyrics by OSCAR HAMMERSTEIN II
Music by RICHARD RODGERS

Slowly

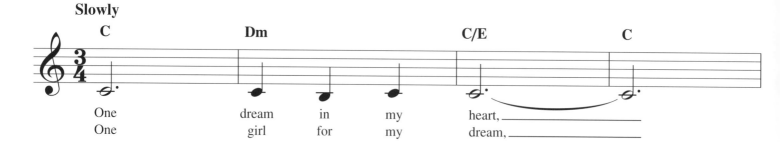

One dream in my heart,
One girl for my dream,

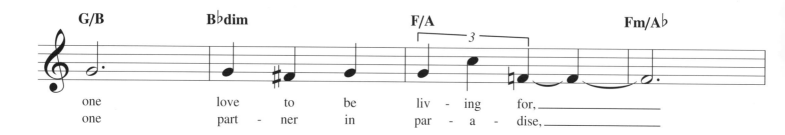

one love to be liv - ing for,
one part - ner in par - a - dise,

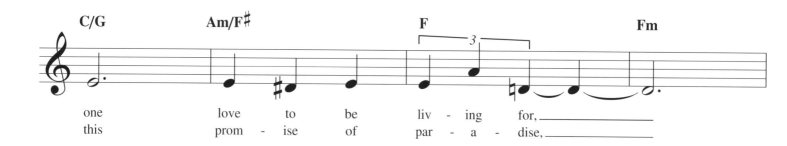

one love to be liv - ing for,
this prom - ise of par - a - dise,

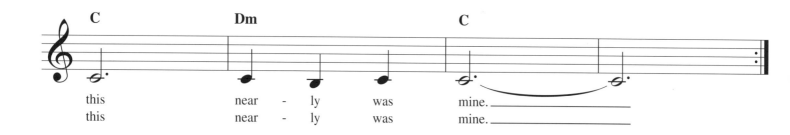

this near - ly was mine.
this near - ly was mine.

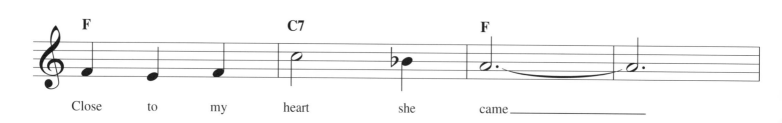

Close to my heart she came

on - ly to fly a - way,

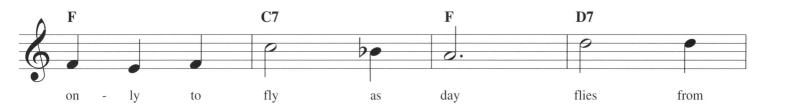

on - ly to fly as day flies from

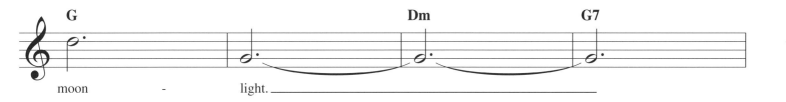

moon - light. _____

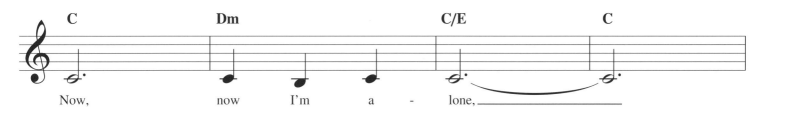

Now, now I'm a - lone, _____

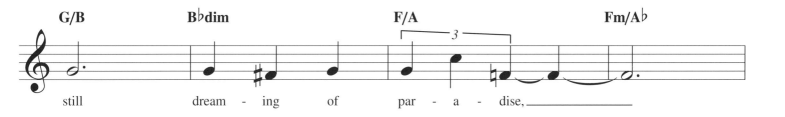

still dream - ing of par - a - dise, _____

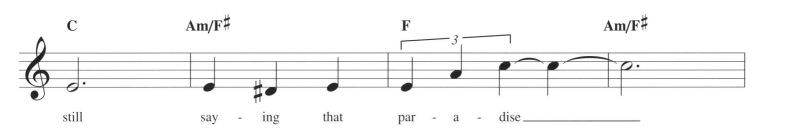

still say - ing that par - a - dise _____

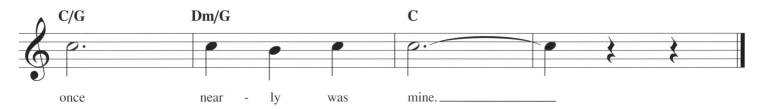

once near - ly was mine. _____

'TIL TOMORROW
from the Musical FIORELLO!

Words by SHELDON HARNICK
Music by JERRY BOCK

Gently

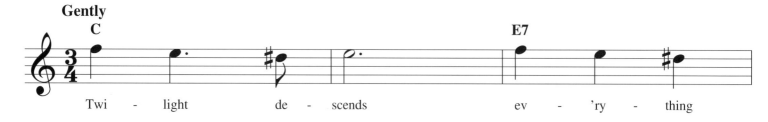

Twi - light de - scends   ev - 'ry - thing

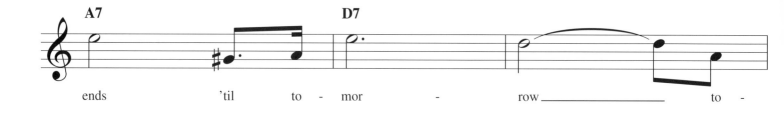

ends   'til to - mor - row _____ to -

mor - row.   Since   we   must

part   here   is   my   heart   'til to -

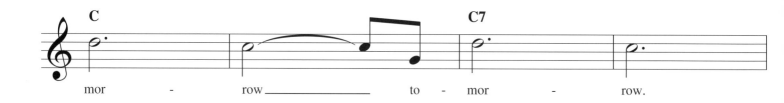

mor - row _____ to - mor - row.

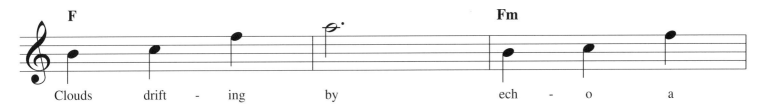

Clouds drift - ing by ech - o a

sigh. Part - ing is such sweet

sor - row. I'm drift - ing

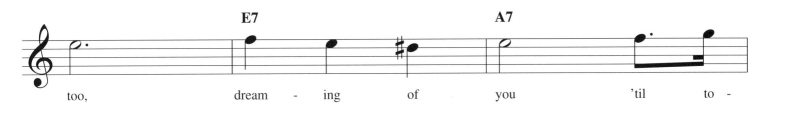

too, dream - ing of you 'til to -

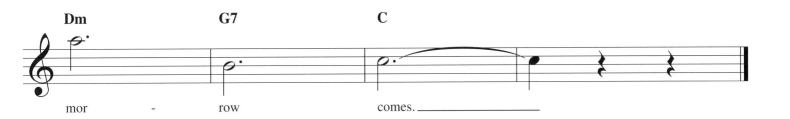

mor - row comes.

TOMORROW
from the Musical Production ANNIE

Lyric by MARTIN CHARNIN
Music by CHARLES STROUSE

Moderately slow

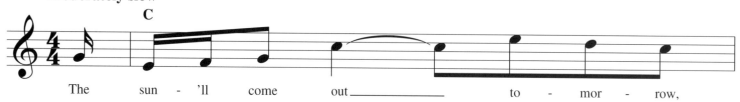

The sun - 'll come out _____ to - mor - row,

bet your bot - tom dol - lar that to - mor-row _____ there'll be

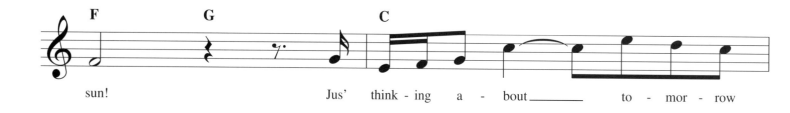

sun!   Jus' think - ing a - bout _____ to - mor - row

clears a - way the cob - webs and the sor row _____ till there's

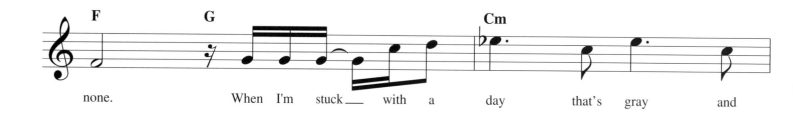

none.   When I'm stuck ___ with a day that's gray and

lone - ly,   I just stick _____ out my

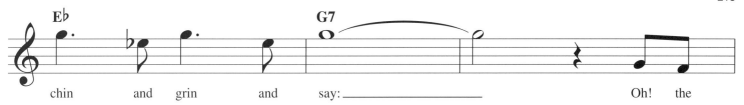

chin and grin and say: _____ Oh! the

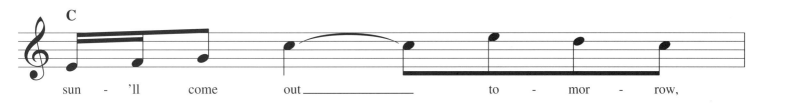

sun - 'll come out_____ to - mor - row,

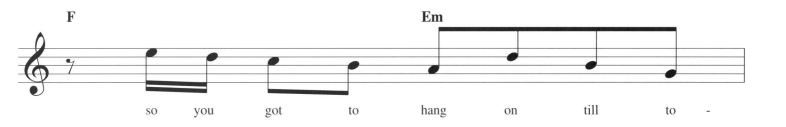

so you got to hang on till to -

mor - row, come what may! To -

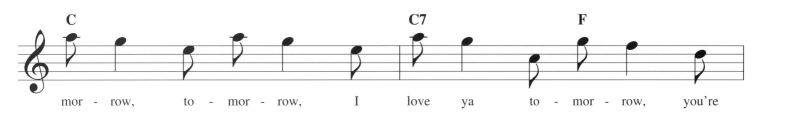

mor - row, to - mor - row, I love ya to - mor - row, you're

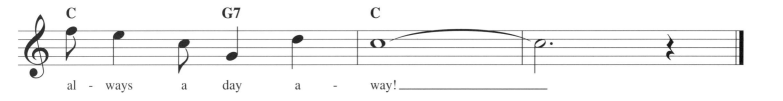

al - ways a day a - way!_____

TOO CLOSE FOR COMFORT
from the Musical MR. WONDERFUL

Words and Music by JERRY BOCK,
LARRY HOLOFCENER and GEORGE WEISS

Medium Swing

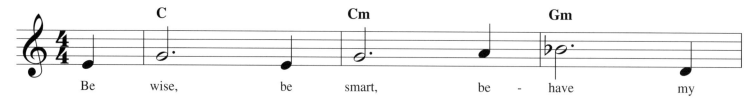

Be   wise,   be   smart,   be - have   my

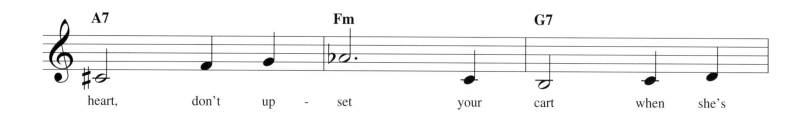

heart,   don't   up - set   your   cart   when   she's

so   close.____   Be   soft,   be

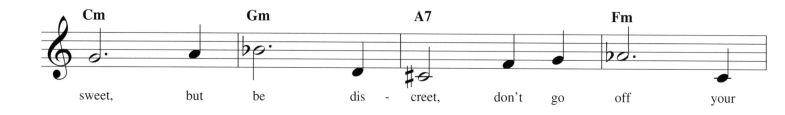

sweet,   but   be   dis - creet,   don't   go   off   your

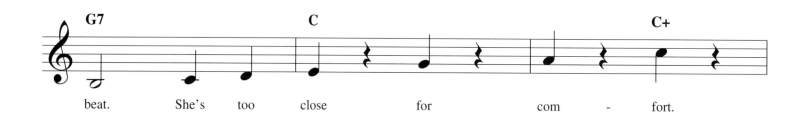

beat.   She's   too   close   for   com - fort.

Too   close,   too____   close   for   com - fort,   please   not   a - gain.__

Too close, too _____ close to know just

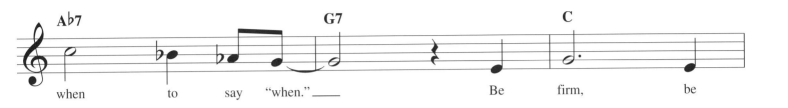

when to say "when." _____ Be firm, be

fair, be sure, be - ware, on your

guard, take care while there's such temp -

ta - tion. One thing leads _____ to an - oth - er,

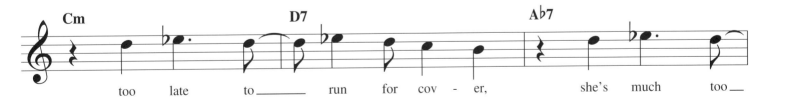

too late to _____ run for cov - er, she's much too _____

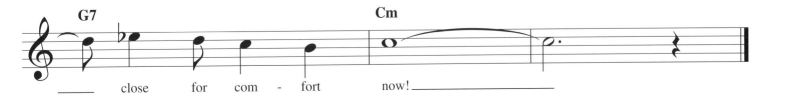

_____ close for com - fort now! _____

WAIT TILL YOU SEE HER
from BY JUPITER

Words by LORENZ HART
Music by RICHARD RODGERS

Moderately

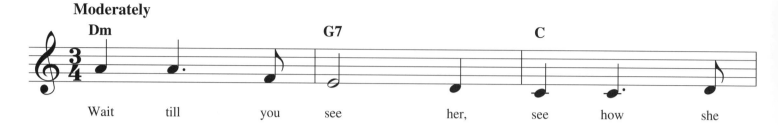

Wait till you see her, see how she

looks, wait till you hear her

laugh._____ Paint - ers of

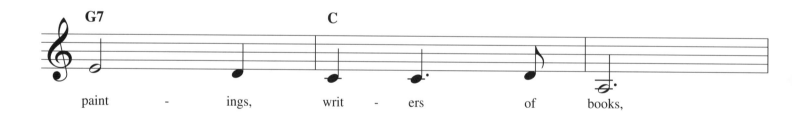

paint - ings, writ - ers of books,

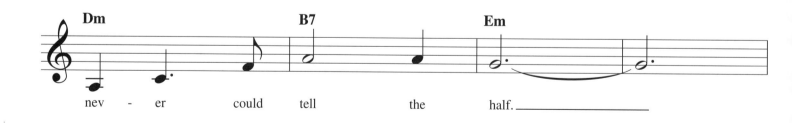

nev - er could tell the half._____

Wait till you feel the warmth of her

glance, pen - sive and sweet and wise._____

_____ All of it love - ly,

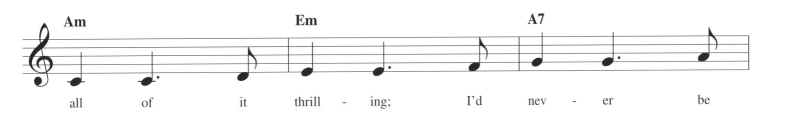

all of it thrill - ing; I'd nev - er be

will - ing to free her,

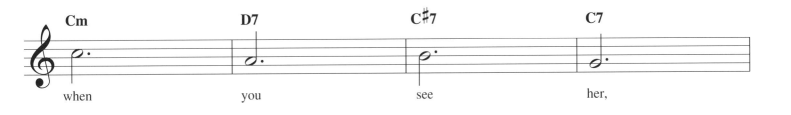

when you see her,

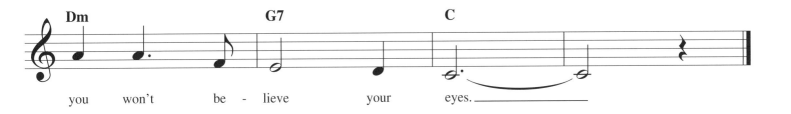

you won't be - lieve your eyes._____

WHEN I'M NOT NEAR THE GIRL I LOVE
from FINIAN'S RAINBOW

Words by E.Y. HARBURG
Music by BURTON LANE

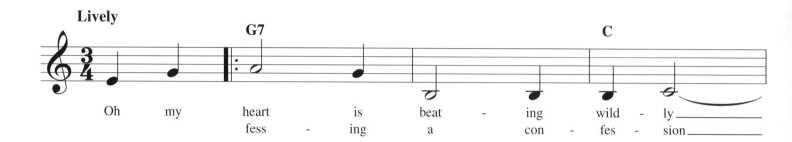

Oh my heart is beat - ing wild - ly _____
fess - ing a con - fes - sion _____

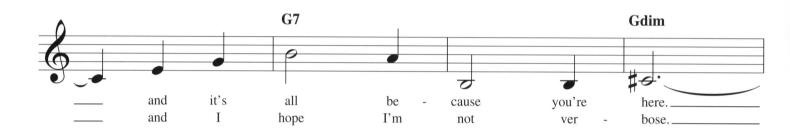

_____ and it's all be - cause you're here. _____
_____ and I hope I'm not ver - bose. _____

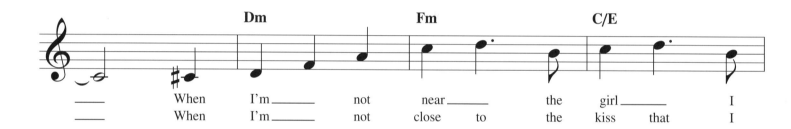

_____ When I'm _____ not near _____ the girl _____ I
_____ When I'm _____ not close to the kiss that I

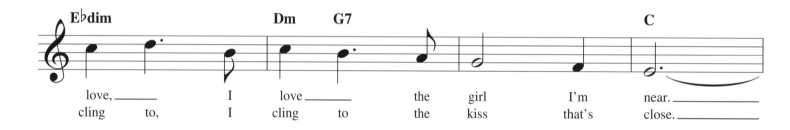

love, _____ I love _____ the girl I'm near. _____
cling to, I cling to the kiss that's close. _____

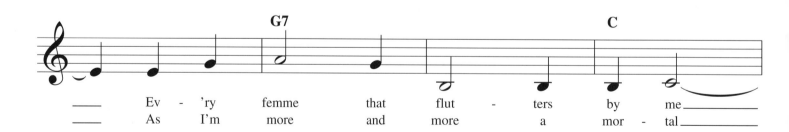

_____ Ev - 'ry femme that flut - ters by me _____
_____ As I'm more and more a mor - tal _____

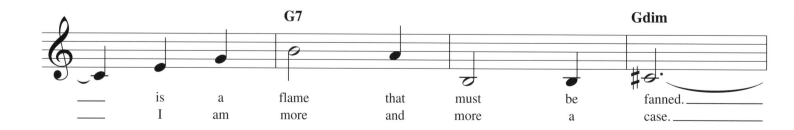

_____ is a flame that must be fanned. _____
_____ I am more and more a case. _____

WHO?
from SUNNY

Lyrics by OTTO HARBACH and OSCAR HAMMERSTEIN II
Music by JEROME KERN

Brightly

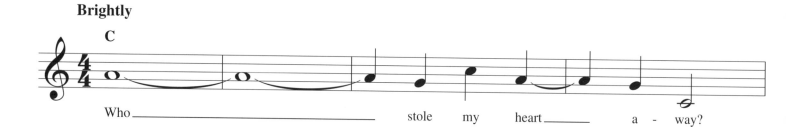

Who _____ stole my heart ___ a - way?

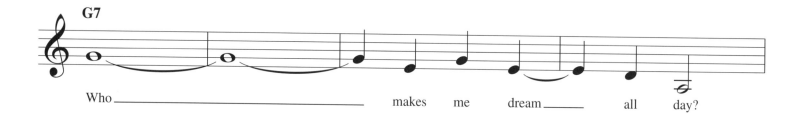

Who _____ makes me dream ___ all day?

Dreams I know, can nev - er be true ___ seems as

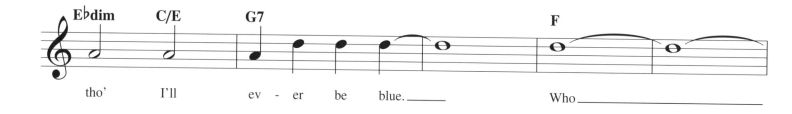

tho' I'll ev - er be blue. ___ Who _____

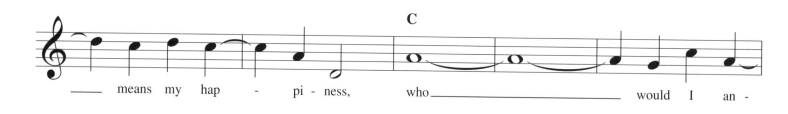

___ means my hap - pi - ness, who _____ would I an -

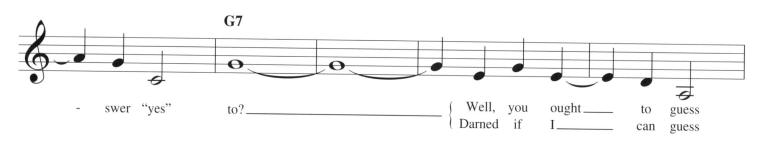

- swer "yes" to? _____ Well, you ought ___ to guess
Darned if I ___ can guess

who,
who,
no one but you! ___

WHY DO I LOVE YOU?
from SHOW BOAT

Lyrics by OSCAR HAMMERSTEIN II
Music by JEROME KERN

Tenderly

Why do I love you? Why do you love me?

Why should there be two hap-py as we?_____

Can you see_____ the why or where - fore, I should be_____

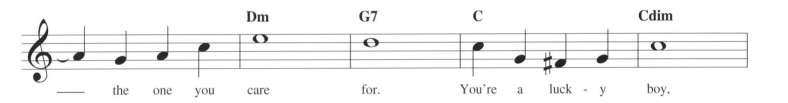

_____ the one you care for. You're a luck - y boy,

I am luck - y too. All our dreams of joy

seem to come true._____ May - be that's_____ be - cause you love

me. May - be that's why I love you!_____

WILLKOMMEN
from the Musical CABARET

Words by FRED EBB
Music by JOHN KANDER

With spirit

Will - kom - men! Bein - ve - nue! Wel - come! _____

Frem - der, e - tran - ger, stran - ger, _____

glück - lich zu se - hen. Je suis en - chan - té. _____

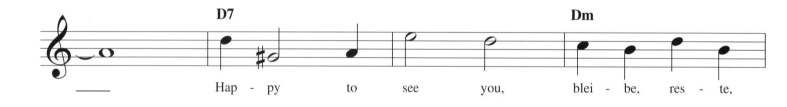

_____ Hap - py to see you, blei - be, res - te,

stay. Will - kom - men! Bien - ve - nue! Wel - come!

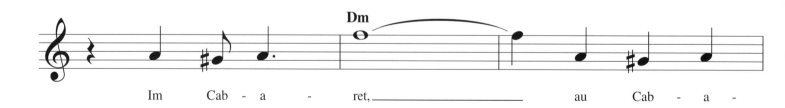

Im Cab - a - ret, _____ au Cab - a -

ret to Cab - a - ret! _____

WITH ONE LOOK
from SUNSET BOULEVARD

Music by ANDREW LLOYD WEBBER
Lyrics by DON BLACK and CHRISTOPHER HAMPTON,
with contributions by AMY POWERS

Slowly

With one look I can break your heart, with one look I play

ev - ery part. I can make your sad heart sing, with one

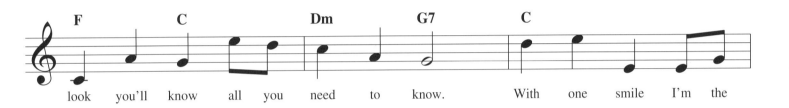

look you'll know all you need to know. With one smile I'm the

girl next door or the love that you've hun - gered for.

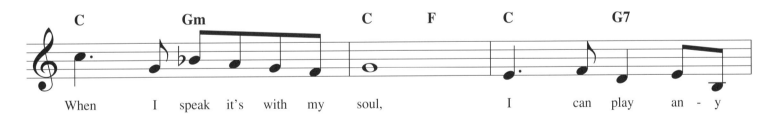

When I speak it's with my soul, I can play an - y

role. No words can tell the sto - ries my eyes tell, watch me

when I frown, you can't write that down. You

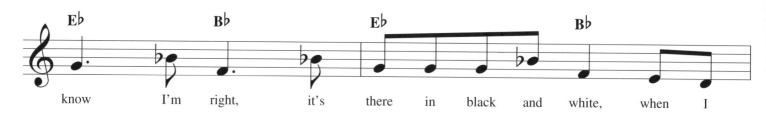

know   I'm   right,   it's   there   in   black   and   white,   when   I

look   your   way   you'll   hear   what   I   say.   Yes,   with   one   look   I   put

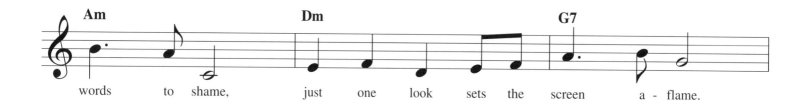

words   to   shame,   just   one   look   sets   the   screen   a - flame.

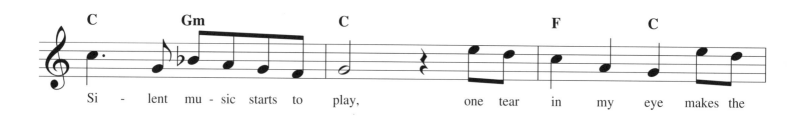

Si - lent   mu - sic   starts   to   play,   one   tear   in   my   eye   makes   the

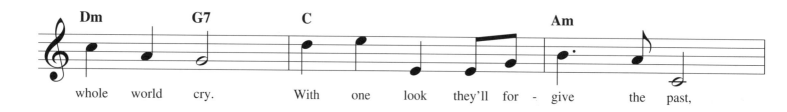

whole   world   cry.   With   one   look   they'll   for - give   the   past,

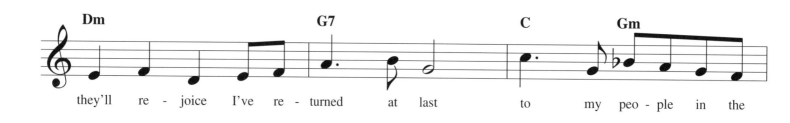

they'll   re - joice   I've   re - turned   at   last   to   my   peo - ple   in   the

dark,   still   out   there   in   the   dark.

225

(Instrumental)

Si - lent mu - sic starts to play. With one

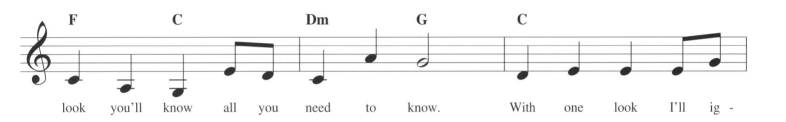
look you'll know all you need to know. With one look I'll ig -

nite a blaze, I'll re - turn to my glo - ry days.

They'll say Nor - ma's back at last. This time I am stay - ing, I'm

stay - ing for good, I'll be back where I was born to be, with

one look I'll be me.

A WONDERFUL DAY LIKE TODAY
from THE ROAR OF THE GREASEPAINT – THE SMELL OF THE CROWD

Words and Music by LESLIE BRICUSSE
and ANTHONY NEWLEY

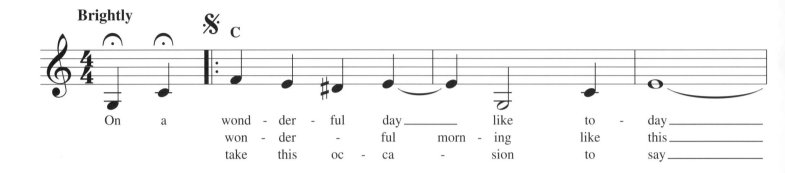
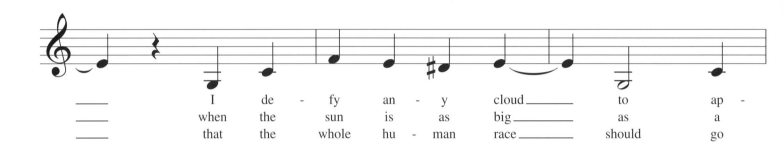

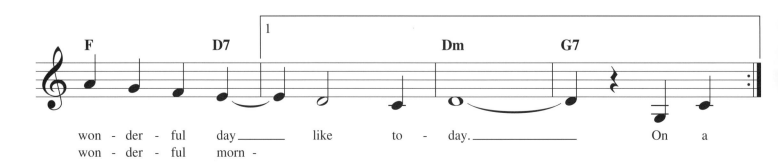

WRITTEN IN THE STARS
from Elton John and Tim Rice's AIDA

Music by ELTON JOHN
Lyrics by TIM RICE

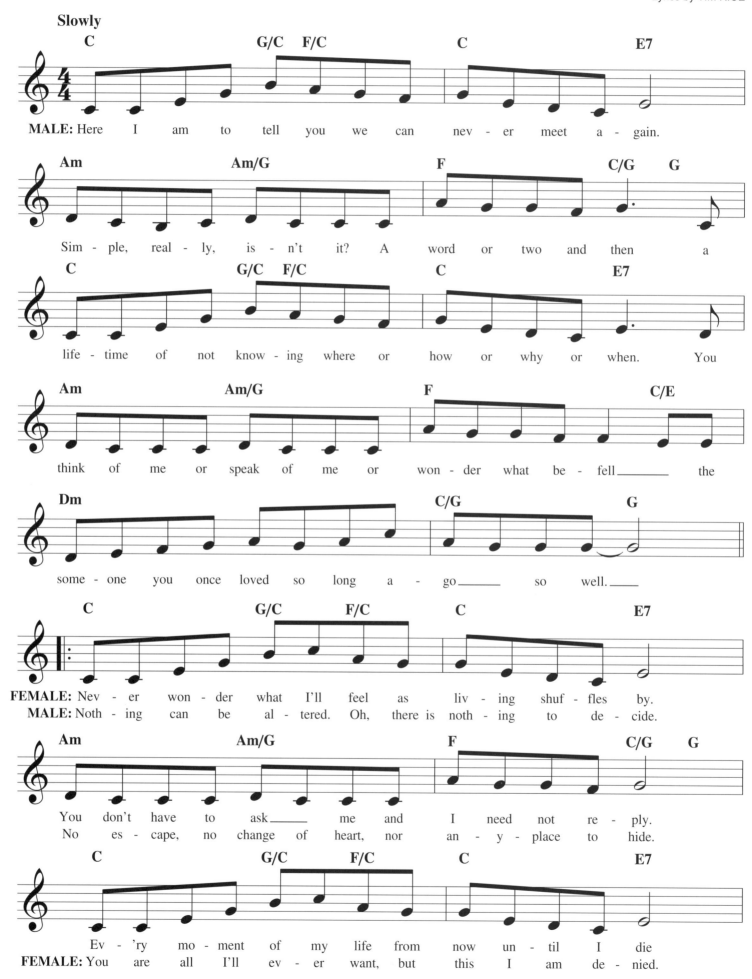

YOU ARE BEAUTIFUL
from FLOWER DRUM SONG

Lyrics by OSCAR HAMMERSTEIN II
Music by RICHARD RODGERS

Moderately

You are beau - ti - ful, small and

shy. You are the girl whose eyes met mine

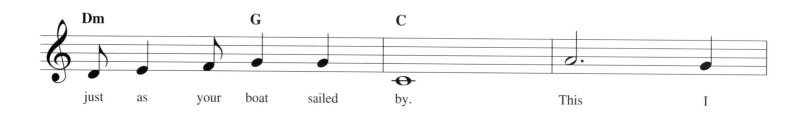

just as your boat sailed by. This I

know of you, noth - ing more.

You are the girl whose eyes met mine

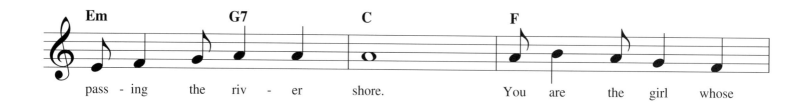

pass - ing the riv - er shore. You are the girl whose

231

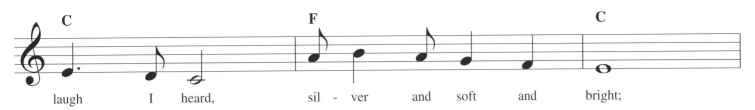

laugh I heard, sil - ver and soft and bright;

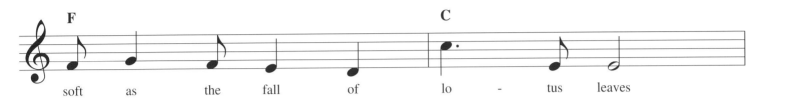

soft as the fall of lo - tus leaves

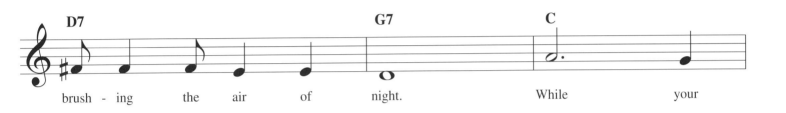

brush - ing the air of night. While your

flow - er boat sailed a - way,

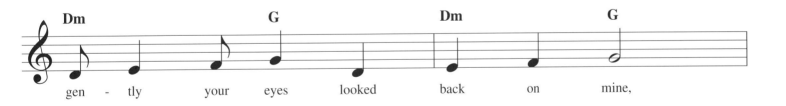

gen - tly your eyes looked back on mine,

clear - ly you heard me say: "You are the girl I will

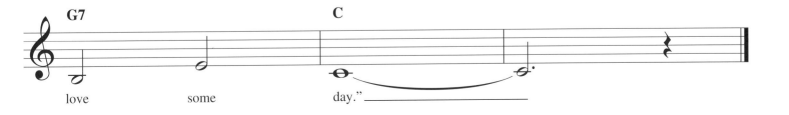

love some day." _____

YOU'RE THE CREAM IN MY COFFEE
from HOLD EVERYTHING

Words and Music by B.G. DeSYLVA,
LEW BROWN and RAY HENDERSON

Moderately

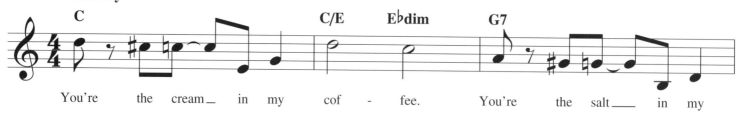

You're the cream in my cof-fee. You're the salt in my

stew. You will al-ways be my ne-ces-si-ty,

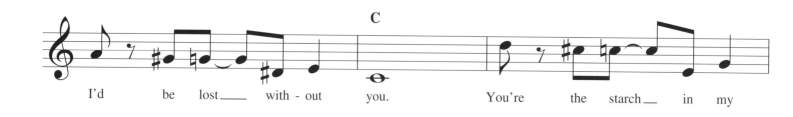

I'd be lost with-out you. You're the starch in my

col-lar, you're the lace in my shoe.

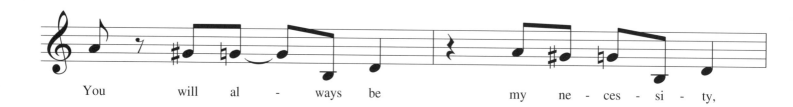

You will al-ways be my ne-ces-si-ty,

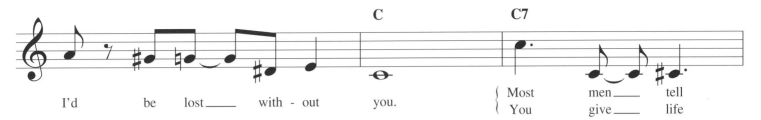

I'd be lost___ with - out you.

C **C7**

Most men___ tell
You give___ life

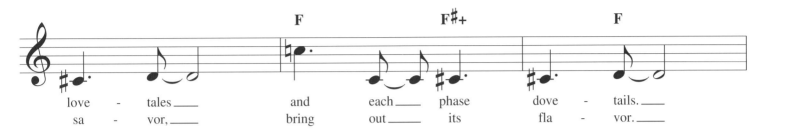

F **F#+** **F**

love - tales___ and each___ phase dove - tails.___
sa - vor,___ bring out___ its fla - vor.___

D7 **Dm** **D7**

You've heard___ each known way, this way___ is___
So this___ is clear, dear, you're my___ Wor -

G7 **C**

___ my own___ way.
- cester - shire,___ dear.

You're the sail___ of my

C/E **Ebdim** **G7**

love - boat you're the cap - tain and crew.

You will al - ways be my ne - ces - si - ty

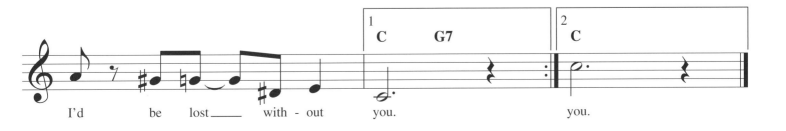

1
C **G7**

2
C

I'd be lost___ with - out you. you.

CHORD SPELLER

C chords

C	C–E–G
Cm	C–Eb–G
C7	C–E–G–Bb
Cdim	C–Eb–Gb
C+	C–E–G#

C# or Db chords

C#	C#–F–G#
C#m	C#–E–G#
C#7	C#–F–G#–B
C#dim	C#–E–G
C#+	C#–F–A

D chords

D	D–F#–A
Dm	D–F–A
D7	D–F#–A–C
Ddim	D–F–Ab
D+	D–F#–A#

Eb chords

Eb	Eb–G–Bb
Ebm	Eb–Gb–Bb
Eb7	Eb–G–Bb–Db
Ebdim	Eb–Gb–A
Eb+	Eb–G–B

E chords

E	E–G#–B
Em	E–G–B
E7	E–G#–B–D
Edim	E–G–Bb
E+	E–G#–C

F chords

F	F–A–C
Fm	F–Ab–C
F7	F–A–C–Eb
Fdim	F–Ab–B
F+	F–A–C#

F# or Gb chords

F#	F#–A#–C#
F#m	F#–A–C#
F#7	F#–A#–C#–E
F#dim	F#–A–C
F#+	F#–A#–D

G chords

G	G–B–D
Gm	G–Bb–D
G7	G–B–D–F
Gdim	G–Bb–Db
G+	G–B–D#

G# or Ab chords

Ab	Ab–C–Eb
Abm	Ab–B–Eb
Ab7	Ab–C–Eb–Gb
Abdim	Ab–B–D
Ab+	Ab–C–E

A chords

A	A–C#–E
Am	A–C–E
A7	A–C#–E–G
Adim	A–C–Eb
A+	A–C#–F

Bb chords

Bb	Bb–D–F
Bbm	Bb–Db–F
Bb7	Bb–D–F–Ab
Bbdim	Bb–Db–E
Bb+	Bb–D–F#

B chords

B	B–D#–F#
Bm	B–D–F#
B7	B–D#–F#–A
Bdim	B–D–F
B+	B–D#–G

Important Note: A slash chord (C/E, G/B) tells you that a certain bass note is to be played under a particular harmony. In the case of C/E, the chord is C and the bass note is E.

THE EASY FAKE BOOK SERIES

100 songs from your favorite decades of music

This series of beginning fake books for players new to "faking" includes:
- 100 memorable songs, all in the key of C
- Lyrics
- Chords which have been simplified, but remain true to each tune
- Easy-to-read, large music notation

THE EASY FORTIES FAKE BOOK

This '40s edition includes: Ac-cent-tchu-ate the Positive • The Anniversary Waltz • Be Careful, It's My Heart • Bésame Mucho (Kiss Me Much) • Bewitched • Boogie Woogie Bugle Boy • Come Rain or Come Shine • Don't Get Around Much Anymore • Easy Street • Frenesí • Harlem Nocturne • Have I Told You Lately That I Love You • How High the Moon • I Got It Bad and That Ain't Good • I'll Remember April • I'm Beginning to See the Light • It Could Happen to You • Java Jive • Love Letters • Mairzy Doats • Moonlight in Vermont • A Nightingale Sang in Berkeley Square • On a Slow Boat to China • Sentimental Journey • Stella by Starlight • The Surrey with the Fringe on Top • Tangerine • You'd Be So Nice to Come Home To • You're Nobody 'til Somebody Loves You • and dozens more.
00240252 Melody/Lyrics/Chords...$19.95

THE EASY FIFTIES FAKE BOOK

Includes: All I Have to Do Is Dream • At the Hop • Beyond the Sea • Blueberry Hill • Chantilly Lace • Don't Be Cruel (To a Heart That's True) • Dream Lover • Earth Angel • Great Balls of Fire • Heartbreak Hotel • Jambalaya (On the Bayou) • Kansas City • La Bamba • Love and Marriage • Love Me Tender • Magic Moments • Mister Sandman • Mona Lisa • Peggy Sue • Put Your Head on My Shoulder • Que Sera, Sera (Whatever Will Be, Will Be) • Rock Around the Clock • Sea of Love • Sh-Boom (Life Could Be a Dream) • Sixteen Candles • Smoke Gets in Your Eyes • Splish Splash • Tennessee Waltz • Unchained Melody • You Belong to Me • Your Cheatin' Heart • and dozens more.
00240255 Melody/Lyrics/Chords...$19.95

THE EASY SIXTIES FAKE BOOK

100 songs from the '60s: Along Comes Mary • Baby Love • Barbara Ann • Born to Be Wild • Brown Eyed Girl • California Girls • Call Me • Dancing in the Street • Do Wah Diddy Diddy • Do You Know the Way to San Jose • The Girl from Ipanema • Good Vibrations • A Groovy Kind of Love • Happy Together • Hey Jude • I Can't Help Myself (Sugar Pie, Honey Bunch) • I Heard It Through the Grapevine • Leader of the Pack • Leaving on a Jet Plane • Louie, Louie • Magic Carpet Ride • Moon River • Respect • (Sittin' On) The Dock of the Bay • Soul Man • Strangers in the Night • Sweet Caroline • Turn! Turn! Turn! • The Twist • Yesterday • and more.
00240253 Melody/Lyrics/Chords...$19.95

THE EASY SEVENTIES FAKE BOOK

Songs from the '70s edition include: Ain't No Mountain High Enough • American Pie • Angie • Baby, I Love Your Way • Bad, Bad Leroy Brown • The Boys Are Back in Town • Come Sail Away • Crocodile Rock • Drift Away • Fame • Free Bird • Honesty • I Will Survive • I'll Never Love This Way Again • Joy to the World • Let It Be • Rainy Days and Mondays • Reeling in the Years • She Believes in Me • Stayin' Alive • Take a Chance on Me • Take Me Home, Country Roads • We Are the Champions • Wonderful Tonight • Y.M.C.A. • You Are So Beautiful • You've Got a Friend • dozens more.
00240256 Melody/Lyrics/Chords...$19.95

Visit Hal Leonard online at **www.halleonard.com** for complete songlists and more.

FOR MORE INFORMATION, SEE YOUR LOCAL MUSIC DEALER,
OR WRITE TO:

HAL•LEONARD® CORPORATION
7777 W. BLUEMOUND RD. P.O. BOX 13819 MILWAUKEE, WI 53213

Prices, contents and availability subject to change without notice.

THE ULTIMATE BROADWAY FAKE BOOK 4TH EDITION

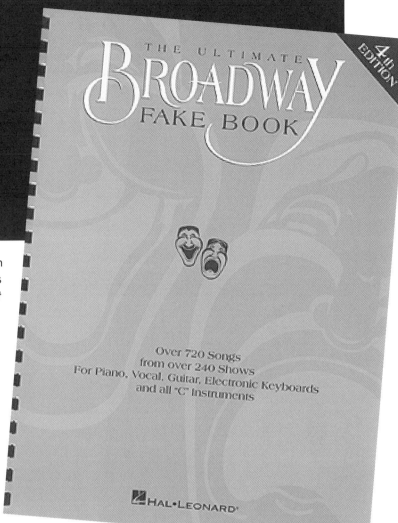

Over 600 pages offering 729 songs from more than 200 Broadway shows! Recently revised to include hits from *Jekyll & Hyde, Martin Guerre, Rent, Sunset Boulevard, Victor/Victoria,* and more! This is the definitive collection of Broadway music, featuring: • Song title index • Show title index • Composer & lyricist index • Synopses of each show.

SONGS INCLUDE:

After You've Gone • Ain't Misbehavin' • All I Ask of You • All of You • All the Things You Are • Angel of Music • Another Op'nin' Another Show • Another Suitcase in Another Hall • Any Dream Will Do • As If We Never Said Goodbye • As Long as He Needs Me • At the Ballet • Bali Ha'i • The Ballad of Sweeney Todd • Beauty and the Beast • Beauty School Dropout • Bess, You Is My Woman • Bewitched • Blue Skies • Bring Him Home • Brotherhood of Man • Buenos Aires • Cabaret • Camelot • Can't Help Lovin' Dat Man • Caravan • Castle on a Cloud • Comedy Tonight • Consider Yourself • Dance: Ten; Looks: Three • Day by Day • Do I Hear a Waltz? • Do-Re-Mi • Do You Hear the People Sing? • Don't Cry for Me Argentina • Down in the Depths (On the Ninetieth Floor) • Easter Parade • Edelweiss • Everything's Coming up Roses • Ev'ry Time We Say Goodbye • Getting to Know You • Give My Regards to Broadway • Guys and Dolls • Have You Met Miss Jones? • Heat Wave • Hello, Dolly! • Hey, Look Me Over • How Are Things in Glocca Morra • How High the Moon • I Can Dream, Can't I? • I Could Have Danced All Night • I Don't Know How to Love Him • I Dreamed a Dream • I Remember It Well • I Won't Grow Up • I've Grown Accustomed to Her Face • If Ever I Would Leave You • If I Can't Love Her • If I Were a Man • If I Were a Rich Man • The Impossible Dream • It's the Hard-Knock Life • June Is Bustin' out All Over • Kids! • La Cage Aux Folles • The Lady Is a Tramp • Lambeth Walk • Last Night of the World • Let Me Entertain You • A Little Night Music • Living in the Shadows • Lost in the Stars • Love Changes Everything • Luck Be a Lady • Make Someone Happy • Makin' Whoopee! • Mame • Maria • Me and My Girl • Memory • Mood Indigo • The Music of the Night • My Funny Valentine • My Heart Belongs to Daddy • A New Life • Oh, What a Beautiful Mornin' • Oklahoma • Ol' Man River • On a Clear Day (You Can See Forever) • On My Own • On Your Toes • One • One Night in Bangkok • Only You • Paris by Night • The Party's Over • People • People Will Say We're in Love • Phantom of the Opera • Quiet Night • The Rain in Spain • Satin Doll • Send in the Clowns • Seventy-Six Trombones • Shall We Dance? • Smoke Gets in Your Eyes • So in Love • Some Enchanted Evening • Someone • Someone like You • The Sound of Music • Standing on the Corner • Starlight Express • Summer Nights • Sun and Moon • Sunrise, Sunset • The Surrey with the Fringe on Top • Tell Me on a Sunday • Tell Me to Go • Thank Heaven for Little Girls • There's No Business like Show Business • This Is the Moment • Tomorrow • Too Darn Hot • Tradition • Try to Remember • Unexpected Song • Waitin' for the Light to Shine • What I Did for Love • Wishing You Were Somehow Here Again • With One Look • You'll Never Walk Alone • and more!

00240046 . . . . **$45.00**

Prices, contents, and availability subject to change without notice.

FOR MORE INFORMATION, SEE YOUR LOCAL MUSIC DEALER,
OR WRITE TO:

HAL•LEONARD CORPORATION

7777 W. BLUEMOUND RD. P.O. BOX 13819 MILWAUKEE, WI 53213